WILDERNESS SURVIVAL SKILLS FOR BEGINNERS

WILDERNESS
SURVIVAL
SKILLS FOR BEGINNERS

The Step-by-Step Guide to Survive the Great Outdoors

JASON MARSTEINER

FOREWORD BY GLENN WELLS

callisto
publishing
an imprint of Sourcebooks

Published by Callisto Publishing LLC C/O Sourcebooks LLC
P.O. Box 4410, Naperville, Illinois 60567-4410
(630) 961-3900
callistopublishing.com

Originally published as *Wilderness Survival Guide: Practical Skills for the Outdoor Adventurer* in 2021 in the United States of America by Callisto, an imprint of Callisto Publishing.

Library of Congress Cataloging-in-Publication Data is on file with the publisher.

Printed and bound in China.
OGP 10 9 8 7 6 5 4 3 2 1

*This book is dedicated to my students
who have spent time with me in the woods.
The best way to learn is to teach.*

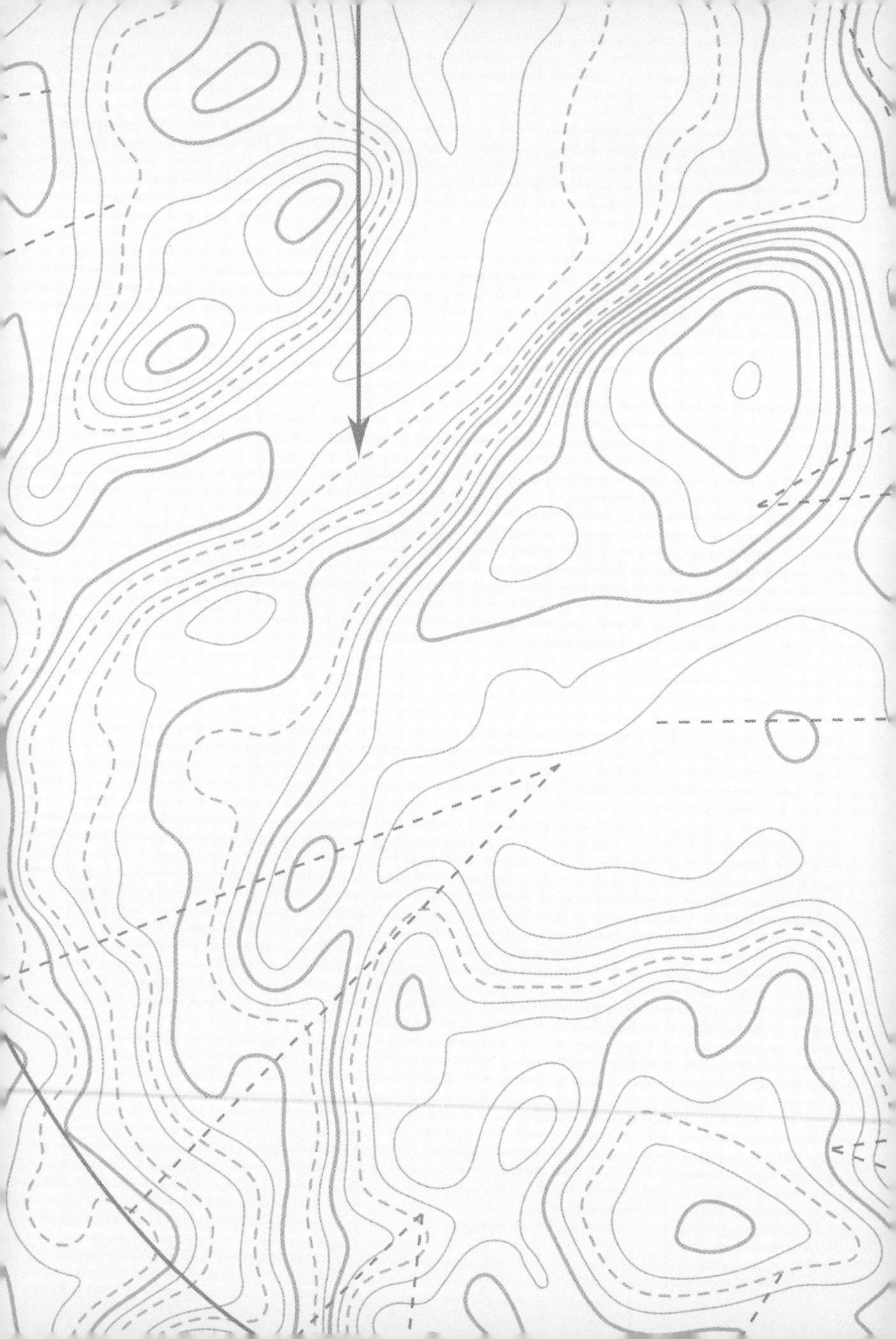

CONTENTS

FOREWORD

I joined the Marine Corps in 1995 and served for 21 years. During that time, I was in the Infantry, Force Reconnaissance, and Marine Special Operations Command as a Raider. Throughout my time in the Marine Corps—and through other sniper and Survival, Evasion, Resistance, and Escape (SERE) training—I became an expert at surviving in many environments and conditions. I have fine-tuned these skills in countries around the world. I retired in 2016, turning my focus to academia. However, I continue to keep my skills fresh by teaching small groups and pushing myself on extended solo and group wilderness outings.

As I read this book, I was pleasantly reminded that, in spite of years of training, I still have a lot to learn. Whether you are a novice or an expert, this book has something valuable to teach you. Something that may end up saving your life, or someone else's. Additionally, this book will boost your confidence and help make your adventures more pleasant.

Jason Marsteiner is precisely what I hope for in an author of a survival book. Jason is a father and a husband, hunter, fisherman, hiker, and camper—identities that many of us share. His advice is educational and practical, unlike that in some survival books whose authors have unrealistic expectations of the reader. Jason has the expertise to educate those who want to have safe hiking and camping adventures and to inform those who want to test their skills as survivalists.

If I can learn something from this book, so can you. This book was written for the beginner as well as for someone like me—an expert with 20 years of experience in survival. Whoever you are, reading and practicing the skills in this book will make you better prepared for a plethora of situations and environments.

Glenn Wells, JD, MSOL
USMC Retired

MEET YOUR GUIDE

Hello, I am Jason Marsteiner, the founder and lead instructor of Colorado Mountain Man Survival LLC and The Survival University, where I teach wilderness survival skills to people of all ages and backgrounds. As the owner and operator of this popular training school, located in the mountains of Colorado, my campus offers thousands of acres of beautiful land to facilitate courses and wilderness immersion retreats. I facilitate public and private courses and welcome families, outdoor adventurers, corporate professionals, Special Forces, active-duty military and retired Veterans.

I am certified as a Wilderness First Responder through Off Grid Medic LLC and hold a Level 1 POST (Peace Officer Standards & Training) certification for search and rescue tracking. Even though the skills I teach are influenced both by primitive and modern survival techniques, the focus of my courses embraces the practical techniques for real-life situations.

I was born at the United States Air Force Academy, in Colorado Springs, Colorado, and grew up in a nearby mountain town where survival skills were a way of life, especially during the winters. As a hunter, fisherman, hiker, camper, craftsman, backyard homesteader, adventurer, and cook, I have spent thousands of hours in the backcountry.

With this book, you will acquire practical skills that are useful any time you venture into the outdoors. If you feel inspired by what you learn, I encourage you to take a hands-on course to further develop your training. Gather your friends, your gear, and don't forget your copy of this book and enjoy your time as you venture into wild places.

CHAPTER ONE

BEFORE YOU GO

A prepared adventurer is one who conditions their body and also their mind. No matter how big or small the journey, planning carefully ensures that you will enjoy yourself and that you will be ready should anything go wrong.

Fit for the Wilderness

Before heading out on your adventure, you should be physically and mentally prepared and have the gear necessary to face the challenge. Situational awareness is key. By constantly paying attention to your surroundings, you will sharpen your mind and make better choices. And, if you are reasonably fit, you will be able to react relatively quickly to what your mind sees, which will help you overcome difficult challenges.

Know Thyself

When outdoor adventurers cannot accept their limitations or do not realize that a challenge is beyond their capabilities, they run into trouble. Importantly, you should know yourself and accept your limitations. Ego kills in the backcountry, so do your best to put it aside. Humans can accomplish unbelievable tasks but not without proper planning and conditioning.

Listen to your instincts. If at any point in your journey you feel that something is amiss, stop and assess the task at hand and your current capabilities. Do you have the proper skills, training, physical condition, and gear to continue on? Did something happen for which you were unprepared? Are you injured or too tired to proceed? Mental conditioning for wilderness adventures means understanding that unexpected things happen all the time.

There may be a point at which you will need to turn back or at the very least reconsider Plan A. Changing your plans or deciding that you need to turn back isn't accepting defeat; it just means that you get to return another day to face the challenge again. You shouldn't feel any shame in making the decision to turn back or to simply stop and rest until you are ready to move forward.

If you take a friend or a group of friends with you, you must know their limitations for the safety of everyone in the group. As you prepare, talk to each member of your group about their experience, physical capabilities, and mental comfort levels. Does anyone have bad knees, a bad back, or another issue that could slow them down? Is one of you diabetic, hypoglycemic, or on a crucial medication that must be taken daily? Does anyone have heart or lung issues, or allergies? You must ask these kinds of questions in order to make appropriate preparations.

If you need to have a serious conversation with a friend or adventure partner about their limitations, never do it in a group setting. Take each friend aside, individually, and have this very important conversation. This conversation isn't about making anyone feel bad—it is about being safe. Be mature, realistic, and supportive. If your friend doesn't want to approach the conversation seriously, they cannot go on the adventure with you. It is really that important.

Also be aware of your partner's competitive nature, as well as your own. A little competition can inspire you to do great things, but it can also put you in harm's way.

Once again, do not let your ego get in the way of making wise decisions. Remember, any decision you make impacts others in your group.

Pre-trip Conditioning

A short, spontaneous adventure may not need much physical conditioning, but relatively long hikes or adventures require you to plan ahead and train. When training, focus on exercises that mimic movements that you will be doing during your adventure. All you have to do is figure out what those motions are and work them into your daily routine.

Start conditioning at least eight weeks before your big adventure. Increase your strength in major muscle groups, especially your legs, shoulders, and lower back. A variation of squats, lunges, dead lifts, and abdominal workouts should help you develop this strength. Remember to incorporate stretching and cardio into your regimen as well.

Pack training. Strengthening your core muscles is important if you plan to carry a heavy pack over many miles. One of my favorite ways to condition for carrying a heavy pack is to climb up stairs or steady inclines. Climb straight up and down as well as sideways, moving your downhill leg in front of the other as you push your way up the hill. As your strength progresses, wear your backpack when climbing. Slowly add weight to your pack.

Scrambles. On long hikes, you might need to scramble up or down slopes on your hands and knees. To train, get down on all fours and position your knees under your hips, keeping your knees slightly off the ground. Keep your back flat and crawl forward a few steps. Crawl backward, then change direction and move laterally. To increase the difficulty of this exercise, wear your backpack.

Push-ups and hangs. To strengthen your arms and chest, add incline and decline push-ups to your workout as well as isometric hangs. An isometric hang involves hanging from a bar or branch with your chin above the bar and holding the position for as long as you can.

Preparing to Meet Your Basic Needs

Spontaneous adventures are great, but they are also typically the most dangerous. Not every adventure requires a long planning process, but a few simple preparations will ensure that you keep out of harm's way.

Gear

Always bring the proper gear with you, know how to use each piece you pack, and make sure that each piece fits and is comfortable. Gear needs vary on the basis of fitness level, environment, budget, knowledge, and many other factors. When planning for your trip, always assume that your destination lacks amenities. Plan to have everything that you'll need if your destination has no showers, running water, toilets, electricity, or barbecue or fire pit.

Remember the core survival rule, "The Rule of Threes":

- **People can survive three minutes without air.**

- **People can survive three hours without shelter.**

- **People can survive three days without water.**

- **People can survive three weeks without food.**

Let's break down these rules as they pertain to gear.

Three minutes without air doesn't simply refer to breathing; three minutes without air means oxygen is not getting to your brain through your blood. No blood, no air, no survival. Your most important gear is in your first aid kit. We will discuss the details of what to include in your first aid kit later on in this book.

Three hours without shelter means three hours exposed to extreme elements. Reduce your exposure to the elements with clothing, shelter, and fire. This rule means packing the proper clothing for both expected and unexpected conditions, as well as packing supplies for starting a fire.

Three days without water can easily turn into one day if you are adventuring in high temperatures or physically exerting yourself. To avoid running out of water, your gear should include a water bottle and a way to purify water.

Three weeks without food is a stretch in most situations. If you are doing more than just lying there waiting for rescue, you are going to need food before three weeks is up. Carry food and means for obtaining more food should your supplies run out.

In short, you should always have food, water, shelter, fire, some sort of first aid, and a signal device with you, even for a simple day hike.

Packing Drill!

Grab a small backpack. Taking five minutes or less, walk around your house and grab items that will cover the Rule of Threes. Think outside the box about how to meet these rules. Keep your pack weight under 10 pounds. How did you do?

Food

Moving around outdoors requires a lot of energy. Planning to keep everyone in your party well-fed is not always simple, especially for longer trips into the wilderness.

If I am hiking for a day, I always bring enough food for two days. If I am going to stay out for five days, I pack enough for seven days. You never know when you might be away longer than expected. As you are making your preparations, remember to focus not only on the food you'll eat but also on the tools you'll need to cook it.

Think ahead: How will you procure food should your food supplies run out? Sourcing your food from the wild is no easy task and requires a fair amount of training and research. When it comes to consuming wild plants, never put anything in your mouth unless you are 110 percent sure that you know what it is (identifying wild plants is covered in chapter 5).

Other than wild plants, you can source food through trapping, hunting, and fishing. You will either need to bring modern tools to do so, or you will have to know how to fashion more primitive devices to procure food. You probably won't carry a hunting rifle on every trip, so what can you bring? My number one tool is my knife. With a single knife, I can create various primitive hunting or trapping tools. I also always carry 50 feet of paracord and a survival fishing kit that is small enough to fit in my pocket. You can purchase premade kits or make one yourself. You will learn what to include in your fishing kit later on in this book.

But before you run around trying to catch every animal that moves in the forest, let's talk briefly about proper food planning and bringing food items with you. Carrying nonperishable foods that are high in protein, complex carbs, and healthy fats is a wise decision. If you are going on a day hike, bringing fresh fruits and vegetables is fine, but you should always have a solid supply of nonperishables in your pack.

Prepare to Be Prepared

Hope for the best, but prepare for the worst. "Lost proof-ing" is the top priority when it comes to planning an adventure. Before you even begin to pack your bag or step out your front door, you should lost proof yourself, by which I mean taking steps to reduce your chances of becoming lost, or to aid rescue teams in finding you if you become lost.

> **STEP 1: LOST PROOFING.** Tell at least one person where you are going, what you are doing, how long you will be gone, with whom you are going, what mode of transportation you are using to start your adventure, and every detail right down to the boots you are wearing. Give your buddy an up-to-date photograph of yourself, your clothes, and your shoes. Do not deviate from your plan. If you must deviate from your plan, contact your person to let them know.
>
> *Sharing information about your shoes with your emergency contact is important because of the tracks they leave. Should you go missing, a good tracking team will find this information valuable. Make a mold of your shoes by pressing them into aluminum foil. Or, take a picture of the soles of your shoes and send that picture to your buddy. If you are making molds of your shoes, take a second mold and leave it in your vehicle along with a map and other written plans for your trip.*

Before I go on a trip, I share my destination and the route I'm taking. If GPS coordinates are available for an area, I send them to my contact's phone. If I know of risky areas, I explain these spots to my person. Caution: If you choose a close loved one as your lost proofer, they may panic should something go wrong and may not immediately remember everything you have told them. Write down everything so that you are not relying on your loved one's memory in a tense moment. Written information can also be more easily shared with search and rescue teams.

STEP 2: CHECK THE WEATHER. Look into not only the projected forecast but also the historical weather trends in your adventure's location. Know when the sun rises, when it sets, and the number of daylight hours. Plan your activities around daylight hours and weather patterns.

STEP 3: ROUTE PLANNING. Study a topographical map of the area where you intend to travel and identify potentially hazardous spots such as cliffs, steep slopes, and other tricky terrain. Identify when you will have to traverse these areas, consider multiple scenarios, and strategize.

STEP 4: GROUP PLANNING. Consider the other people who will be with you. What are their physical limitations, medical needs, skill levels, and outdoor knowledge? Find out the name of their lost proof buddy, their emergency contacts, and what needs to be done should they, or another person in your group, become lost or injured. Do any of you have CPR, first aid, first responder, or wilderness medical training? If so, what are the limits of your training? If you don't have this training, do you think it is important enough to train before you start your adventure?

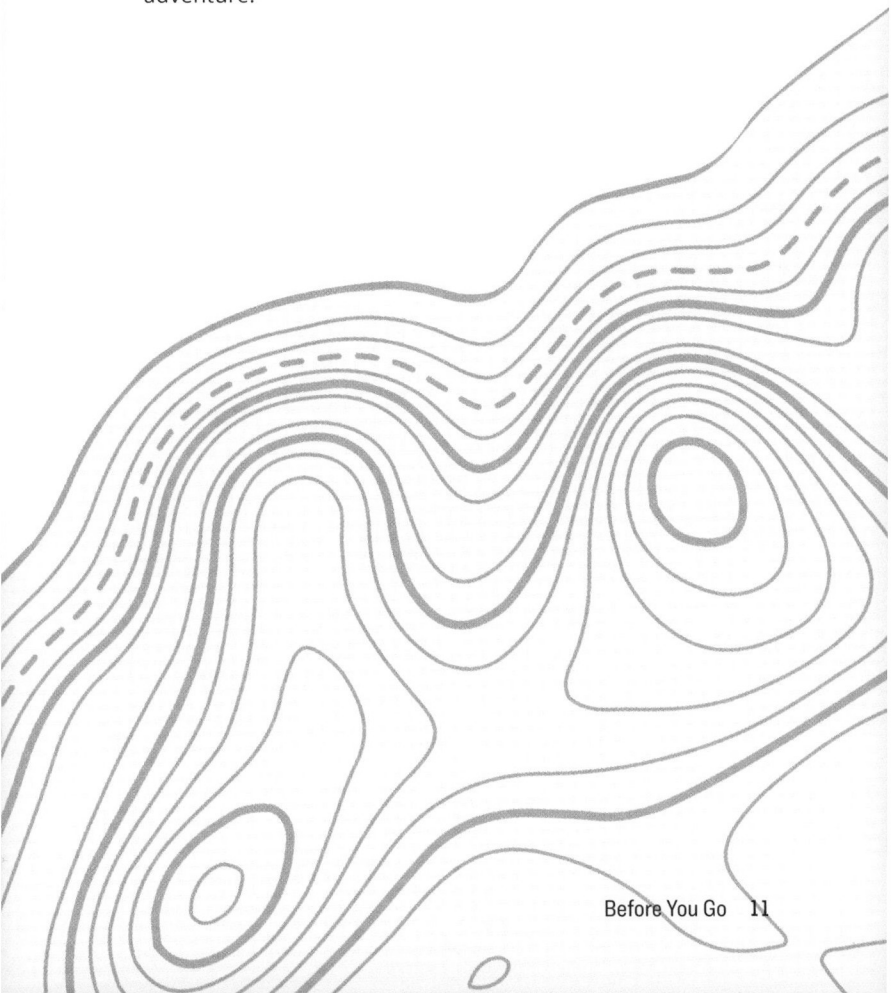

PREPARATION CHECKLIST

☐ Everyone in your party has the physical requirements to match the adventure you have chosen.

☐ You have had a discussion with others about pertinent physical and medical concerns and history.

☐ You have left written documentation of your plans, including a map and route to your destination, as well as recent pictures of yourself and your gear.

☐ You have made an imprint and/or taken pictures of the bottom of your hiking boots.

☐ You have explained your adventure plans in detail to your lost proof buddy.

☐ You have checked the weather forecast and weather history of the area.

☐ You have planned your route using a topographical map and/or other online resources.

☐ Your gear, at minimum, covers the basic survival needs of the Rule of Threes.

☐ Everyone else in your party has their own gear to cover basic survival needs.

☐ You have tested each piece of your gear for durability, practical uses, and comfort.

☐ You have packed the proper amount of food for each day plus an extra day or two to cover the unexpected.

- [ ] You have researched and learned about edible and poisonous plants in the area.

- [ ] You have included tools in your gear to procure food should your packed supplies run out.

- [ ] You have included tools in your gear to use as signaling devices.

- [ ] You have acquired basic first aid training, preferably wilderness first aid training.

- [ ] You have made a contingency plan with your adventure partner about what to do if anyone in your group becomes lost or injured.

- [ ] You have made sure that everyone in your party knows and agrees with your plan.

- [ ] You are mentally prepared to turn around and come home should something not look or feel right.

CHAPTER TWO

THE RIGHT STUFF

To put it simply, a person should not venture out into the wilderness without the basic necessities. You should always have at least the minimum amount of gear to cover your essential survival needs. That said, the quality of your gear counts. In my profession, I commonly hear that having some sort of gear is better than having nothing, but I am a firm believer that this logic is incorrect. Poor-quality gear gives you a false sense of security as it could break when you need it the most. Gear failure in a critical situation can cost you your life. Your gear should be durable and have multiple uses. So, what is the best gear to cover your essential needs?

A big difference stands between what you want and what you need. When you consider your survival, a few core items fall into the "need" category. At the top of the list of your gear needs should be items that are the hardest to re-create in the wilderness. With this idea in mind, the top five items that are the most vital for survival, in order of importance, are:

1. A fixed-blade, full-tang knife, like the one pictured here.

2. A ferrocerium rod (for starting fires), like the one pictured here.

3. A durable poncho (for protection from the elements and, if needed, for use as a shelter).

4. A 40-ounce, single-walled metal canteen, like the one pictured here.

5. Paracord (50 feet on day hikes/100 feet on overnight hikes/200 feet on extended trips)

These five items will provide for your survival priorities, or meet your Rule of Threes. Of course, most of us prefer to carry more than just the absolute bare necessities. The following sections cover items that are also important to have for most wilderness adventurers.

Choosing a Pack

To carry your must-have items, you'll need a good pack. Though many types of packs are available, two primary styles are best for the serious outdoorsperson.

Hiking backpacks. These packs are lightweight and comfortable. Many brands and designs are available; shop around to find a pack to fit your needs. Packs for women adventurers are available, with variations in the straps, weight distribution, and sizes for a better fit. Most hiking packs come with a comfortable waist belt to help disperse the weight of your pack. Most packs are also made out of brightly colored material and can be used for signaling because they can be spotted easily.

The hiking pack has a few drawbacks. As these packs are made out of lightweight material, the fabric is not extremely durable, though the stitching and zippers are strong on quality packs. The brightly colored fabrics can be a pro when you are lost but are a con when you are trying to avoid being spotted, as when hunting. Quality packs also tend to come with a heavy price tag.

Tactical packs. These kinds of packs are very durable, though in general they are not as comfortable as hiking backpacks. Tactical packs include many attachment points (known as MOLLE, or modular lightweight load-carrying equipment), so you can easily attach whatever accessories you might want to the outside of the pack. Tactical packs, like hiking packs, come in a variety of sizes.

Unfortunately, no tactical packs are specifically designed for the female body. The durability of these packs makes them heavy. If weight is a concern, then a tactical backpack will not work for you. Not all tactical packs come with a waist belt, and those that do aren't nearly as comfortable as a hiking bag. A good tactical backpack can also be expensive. Tactical packs tend to be compartmentalized, which can get in the way when carrying a lot of gear. The exception to using a tactical pack to carry a lot of gear is using a large military rucksack, which are specifically designed for this purpose.

Choosing Essential Kits

The following sections discuss the contents of the eight essential kits that you should carry with you. These include:

Tool kit. Fixed-blade knife and other primary tools.

Fire kit. Ignition source and tinder.

Shelter kit. Clothing; something to sleep under, in, and on; sewing/repair; and rope or cordage.

Hydration kit. Water procurement, filtration, purification, and container.

Nutrition kit. Premade food and supplies for food procurement and preparation.

Navigation kit. Map, compass, and ranger beads.

Communications kit. Cell phone, radios, beacons, and signaling devices.

Trauma/first aid kit. Supplies to care for bleeding, respiratory and circulation support, and hypothermia.

Tool Kit

The items in your tool kit don't fall into any of the other kit categories, but these items will help you accomplish tasks related to every one of your other kits. These essential items should be durable and reliable.

Fixed-blade, full-tang knife. A good knife should always be your item number one. Your knife should fit comfortably in your hand, and it should be full tang, which means that the metal making up the knife spans from the tip of the blade all the way down to the end of the handle.

Handsaw, axe, and machete. If necessary, these three items can be replaced by your knife. I would, however, recommend keeping at least a folding handsaw in your pack. A handsaw will help you quickly process firewood or cut down small trees for a shelter.

Multitool. A multitool is a foldable pair of pliers with a tool kit in the handle. It should have wire cutters, a small saw, a good blade, and an awl. You can use this tool to make fishing lures and snare wires, or to repair broken gear. The wire cutters and pliers are invaluable in some medical situations, such as when removing a fishing hook from your body.

Flashlight and headlamp. Your flashlight, headlamp, or both should be rechargeable; otherwise, you will need to carry batteries. Don't forget your solar charger. Everyone in your group should have their own headlamp.

Carabiners and ranger bands. These multifunctional items help secure things to your pack or help you perform other tasks in the field. Ranger bands are thick rubber bands and can be used to splint broken fingers, keep containers closed, improve the grip on knives, and as improvised potholders.

Cordage. Ropes or cords help with tasks like fishing, hunting, shelter building, and climbing. The best cordage for outdoor situations is paracord or bank line. Rated to hold 550 pounds of weight, 550 Paracord consists of an outer sheathing and seven smaller inner strands. It can be pulled apart, so you can use just the sheathing or smaller strands for fishing, sewing, or trap-making.

You may want to add other items to your tool kit depending on where you will be, how long you will be in the wilderness, and the types of activities you will be pursuing. Make your tool kit fit your specific needs.

Fire Kit

You'll need the items in your fire kit to create and sustain fire. If you are an experienced bushcrafter, you may think that you don't need these items because you can start a fire with a bow drill. Not preparing these supplies is an example of ego getting in the way of good decision-making. Although you likely have the knowledge to start a fire without using modern gear, doing so requires an immense amount of effort and should not be your primary means of starting a fire. We will discuss fire-starting techniques in chapter 4.

Ignition source. Lighters and matches are not bad options, but neither works well in high winds or when wet, and they are hard to hold when your hands are cold. Lighters may not work at higher altitudes or when temperatures drop below freezing. You might consider solar ignition sources, although these are unreliable because they require the sun to work. A good primary ignition source is the ferrocerium rod, or ferro rod. Ferrocerium is a pyrophoric metal alloy that can reach temperatures over 5,000°F when rapidly oxidized, which means that when you scrape another piece of metal or your knife across the ferro rod, a really hot spark is produced. One ferrocerium rod can ignite thousands of fires.

Tinder. Tinder includes items that you bring with you to set on fire. You can source your tinder from natural materials, and you should whenever such materials present themselves. But always have a backup in your pack.

A great go-to tinder source is cotton balls and petroleum jelly because they are both cheap and an easy combination to make at home. Place a handful of cotton balls (10 to 20) and 1 heaping tablespoon of petroleum jelly per 10 cotton balls inside a sandwich bag. Thoroughly slather the outside of each cotton ball with petroleum jelly and press the cotton ball in your fist so that the jelly penetrates the surface of the cotton ball. Do not tear the cotton balls apart. Store this premade tinder in a waterproof container or old pill bottle. Other options include dryer lint and petroleum jelly, ranger bands, wood shavings, or fatwood (pine wood impregnated by sap or flammable resin). You can also purchase products like WetFire Tinder.

Shelter Kit

Clothing. Your shelter kit will make up the bulk of your gear and starts with clothing. The most important thing to know for cold weather climates is that cotton kills. Cotton absorbs and retains moisture and loses its insulation value once it's wet, which means that when the temperature drops, you are going to freeze. Keep cotton out of your gear unless you adventure in hot environments, and even then you should have non-cotton backups.

Only one piece of gear in my kit is cotton: my shemagh (a large cotton scarf traditionally worn in the Middle East). The shemagh has some very good uses, including gathering dew off vegetation. You can wear a shemagh as a head wrap to protect yourself from the sun or wind. You can use it as a prefilter for your water filter; a tourniquet, bandage, or arm sling; and a gear or firewood carrier.

Other than my scarf, all of my clothing items are wool or water-wicking synthetic materials. I prefer wool because it's fire resistant and will keep you warm even if you're wet. When dressing for cold or wet weather, use the layering system.

- **Base layer.** Thin, lightweight, water-wicking wool or synthetic fabrics make up your base layer. Think long underwear and socks. This layer should be tight-fitting and should never include cotton.

- **Mid layer.** Garments that are loose-fitting, lightweight fleece, goose down, or wool serve as your insulating mid layer. You see this layer every day. Pants, shirts, sweaters, etc.

- **Outer protective layer.** This durable ventilated layer protects you from wind, rain, or snow. The outer protective layer must have proper ventilation to allow sweat to evaporate and escape without letting in moisture. Your outer layer is your jacket and insulated pants.

- **Outer shell.** Windproof and waterproof, your outer shell is your rain gear and windbreaker.

When selecting your clothing, make certain to have a piece of clothing to cover every inch of your body. Don't forget hats, gloves, and footwear. Clean, dry socks are extremely important, and you should always bring an extra pair with you. Pack a sewing kit so that you can make repairs to small holes or tears that might occur on the trail.

Something to sleep under, in, and on. The rest of your shelter is your sleep system. Your sleep system includes something to sleep under—like a tarp, tent, or rain fly. You will also need something to sleep on to keep you comfortable and insulated from the cold ground. You may use a sleeping pad or a hammock. What you choose to sleep in will depend on how much weight you want to carry as well as the weather and climate of your destination. Options include a sleeping bag, wool blanket, bivy sack, or a sleeping bag liner.

Hydration Kit

This kit includes everything that you need to gather, carry, and make water safe to drink. Keep in mind that water filtration and water purification are two different things. Water filtration removes sediment floating in the water and may make it smell and taste better. Purification removes viruses and bacteria, making your water safer to drink. Boiling purifies your water but does not filter it. You can push your water through sand and charcoal to filter it, but this process does not purify it. We will discuss locating, procuring, and preparing water in chapter 4.

Shemagh or large cotton scarf. Your shemagh also is part of your hydration kit because it can be used to procure water and as a prefilter to extend the life of any filtration/purification system.

Single-walled metal water bottle or canteen. You can boil water directly in a single-walled metal bottle or canteen; you cannot boil water in a plastic or insulated bottle. The CDC recommends you boil water for three minutes to kill any bacteria and/or viruses.

Water purification tablets (chlorine, chlorine dioxide, or iodine-based). These tablets purify water, making it safe to drink. Be sure to follow specific guidelines on the packaging as to how much water each tablet can purify. Purification tablets are not my preference, but I carry them in case of emergency.

Water filter/purifier. Most store-bought water filters are ultrafiltration (UF) water purifiers, so they use pressure to force water through a semipermeable membrane to remove particles, bacteria, and sometimes viruses. When purchasing a water filter, consider packable size, weight, and the micron level of the filter. Several affordable water filters provide 0.1 micron filtration, meaning they filter out 99.99 percent of all bacteria. If you are traveling to an area where viruses are an issue, be sure that your water filter/purifier can also filter out viruses.

Hydration backpack. Hydration packs provide a large storage capacity and make it easy to stay hydrated with a drinking hose at your fingertips. An inline water filter can also be attached to hydration packs, making the filtration process simpler.

Nutrition Kit

This kit includes the food that you bring with you, the items you need to prepare your food, and the items that you need to procure more food in the event your supplies run out.

Cooking supplies. A two-quart cooking pot will enable you to make large meals or stews without spilling the broth that is created. Pack items inside the pot to make the best use of space. Plan to include a lightweight backpacker's stove (compact titanium woodstove or propane stove) in your pack, along with a space-saver cup that fits over the base of your metal water bottle and a spoon, fork, or spork.

Food procurement. To prepare for unforeseen circumstances where your food supplies are lost or depleted, carry a fishing kit (including hooks, fishing line, sinkers, swivels, bobbers, plastic worms, lures, and flies), trapping kit (wire, cables, and locks), and a hunting kit (spearheads and arrowheads). Include paracord and a slingshot with ball bearings (which can be replaced with rocks). We will discuss trapping and fishing in chapter 5.

Navigation Kit

The items that I recommend for your navigation kit are of the low-tech variety. We will discuss finding your way by using these tools in chapter 6.

Topographical map. Most maps sold in outdoor stores have a scale of 1:63,360, where one inch on the map equals one mile on the planet. I find that a better option is a 1:24,000 scale, which provides more detail and is the scale most commonly used by search and rescue. You can print maps from sites like USGS.gov so that you will have a precise map for the location that you intend to visit.

Compass. A good compass is crucial. Opt for either an orienteering compass or a lensatic compass. We will discuss how to use your compass in chapter 6.

Ranger beads. The final tool in a good navigation kit is ranger beads, also known as pace count beads. Ranger beads are used to keep track of the distance you have traveled over land.

Communications Kit

Signaling and communications devices are used to stay in contact with others in your party or to help others find you should you get lost.

Cell phone. Many lost adventurers have decided, for whatever reason, to leave their cell phones behind. I recommend carrying your phone in a waterproof container in your pack when in the backcountry. Even if you have no signal, you may be able to dial 911 or send a text for help.

Two-way radios. If you are traveling with others, you should each have a short-range radio or a walkie-talkie.

Signaling device. Signal devices are either visual or auditory and are designed to get someone's attention. These devices can include signal mirrors, whistles, a flag or other piece of brightly colored material, flares, glow sticks, flashlights, strobes, lasers, survey tape, or permanent markers. Choosing which tools to carry will depend on your personal preference as well as the landscape, time of day, and climate where you will be adventuring.

Personal locator beacon. If you frequent the backcountry often, consider purchasing a personal locator beacon (PLB) or a satellite messenger. For truly remote areas, a PLB is your best option. A PLB will send for help (but can do nothing else), and you will be unable to cancel the signal. Don't hit that button by accident. Satellite messengers are less reliable globally but have other features such as navigation, weather reports, and the ability to send custom messages or post to social media.

Avalanche beacons. If you are a backcountry skier, snowboarder, snowshoer, or extreme winter adventurer, an avalanche beacon is a must, as is a friend to go out with you. Each of you will need to wear a transceiver. Should you be buried in an avalanche, your friend can switch their device to search mode and hopefully locate you quickly.

Trauma/First Aid Kit

In the case of survival, I carry two types of first aid kits: an individual first aid kit (IFAK) and a trauma kit. We will discuss first aid protocols in detail in chapter 7.

Individual first aid kit. An IFAK is far more complex than your typical store-bought first aid kit. An IFAK is small and is primarily intended to provide supplies for the person carrying it. Your IFAK should include:

☐ Trauma shears

☐ PPE: Latex, vinyl, or nitrile gloves; mask; and eye protection

☐ CPR mask

☐ One standard adult-size and one kid-size OPA (oropharyngeal airway)

☐ ×4 Sterile 4×4 sponge or blood absorber

☐ ×2 Gauze pad 4×4

☐ ×2 Rolls of gauze/bandage

☐ ×4 Adhesive bandages

☐ Chest seal

- [ ] Combat application tourniquets (CATs) and stretch-wrap-and-tuck tourniquets (SWAT-Ts)

- [ ] Heavy-duty two-inch surgical tape

- [ ] Any needed medication or prescription

Trauma kit. The trauma kit carries supplies to refill the IFAK and is also meant to be used on other people or for bigger medical emergencies.

Your personal trauma kit will vary greatly depending on your training and packable space allowed. Consider that although you might not be trained, your rescuer might be, and having these supplies in your kit could help them save your life. All of the items on the following list might not fit in your kit, but in an ideal situation, you should have these items. If you can't fit everything in your pack, prioritize your IFAK and carry extra gauze and tape along with some of the smaller items. Acquire training, like a wilderness first-responder class, so that you know how to use each of these items and how to improvise should you not have everything.

- [ ] Notepad and pencil

- [ ] Pulse oximeter

- [ ] Thermometer

- [ ] Stethoscope

- [ ] Blood pressure cuff

- [ ] Collapsible BVM (bag valve mask)

- [ ] Heavy-duty one- and two-inch surgical tape
- [ ] Additional sterile 4×4 sponge or blood absorbers
- [ ] Additional 4×4 gauze pads
- [ ] Additional rolled gauze/bandages
- [ ] "Israeli bandage" (trauma dressing)
- [ ] Hemostatic dressings
- [ ] Additional open-chest seal
- [ ] Structural aluminum malleable (SAM) splint
- [ ] Tweezers
- [ ] Duct tape
- [ ] Needle and thread
- [ ] Additional adhesive bandages
- [ ] Pain relievers (ibuprofen, Tylenol, aspirin, and baby aspirin for blood loss)
- [ ] Antihistamines and cold and cough medicines
- [ ] Antacids and antidiarrheal medicines
- [ ] Antibiotic ointment
- [ ] Salt and sugar packets to make electrolyte drinks
- [ ] Cake frosting in a tube or baggie to address low blood sugar

PACKING LIST FOR SURVIVING IN THE WILD

Must-Haves

- [ ] Full-tang, fixed-blade knife
- [ ] Tinder
- [ ] Sleep system (tarp, sleeping bag, ground pad)
- [ ] IFAK
- [ ] Fishing kit
- [ ] Backpack
- [ ] Ferrocerium rod
- [ ] Lighter
- [ ] Matches (waterproof)
- [ ] Handsaw
- [ ] Tarp/poncho
- [ ] Carabiners
- [ ] Mylar blanket
- [ ] Map (topographic 1:24,000 scale)
- [ ] Compass
- [ ] 550 Paracord (50 feet on day hikes/100 feet on overnight/200 feet on extended trips)
- [ ] Metal canteen (40-ounce, single-walled)
- [ ] Metal space-saver cup
- [ ] Water filter/purifier
- [ ] Headlamp
- [ ] Hiking boots
- [ ] Outdoor clothing (base layer, mid layer, outer layer)
- [ ] Boot gaiters (if traversing through snow)
- [ ] Bandanna/shemagh
- [ ] Rain gear
- [ ] Sewing/repair kit
- [ ] Food

- ☐ Multivitamins
- ☐ Signal whistle

Nice-to-Haves

- ☐ Hatchet/axe
- ☐ Machete
- ☐ Shovel (handheld)
- ☐ Solar charger
- ☐ GPS
- ☐ Locator beacon
- ☐ Radio (two way)
- ☐ Flashlight
- ☐ Spare batteries
- ☐ Two-quart cooking pot
- ☐ Sunscreen/ bug spray
- ☐ Work gloves
- ☐ Trekking poles

- ☐ Multitool
- ☐ Sunglasses
- ☐ Knife sharpener
- ☐ Hydration bladder
- ☐ Hunting kit
- ☐ Signal mirror
- ☐ Signal flare
- ☐ Toilet paper
- ☐ Soap
- ☐ Toothbrush/ toothpaste
- ☐ Resealable bag
- ☐ Trash bag
- ☐ Slingshot
- ☐ Camping stove
- ☐ Duct tape
- ☐ Electrical tape
- ☐ Snowshoes
- ☐ Crampons

CHAPTER THREE

LEARNING THE LAND

Knowing the climate and terrain that you will be traversing is imperative. Your needs and risks vary depending on the land and the weather; plan your trip accordingly.

By studying the climate, you will be better prepared for extreme temperatures, rain, snow, or wind. Whether you are in a polar climate or a tropical one, you could encounter a variety of terrain features, including mountains, valleys, lakes, and rivers. In fact, some terrain features create their own microclimates. You might face a polar climate within a few miles of a mountain ascent that begins in a temperate climate. Every terrain within each climate offers unique resources, benefits, challenges, and dangers. The best way to face climate and terrain challenges is to bring the proper gear and do your homework before you go.

Polar Climates

Polar climates make up less than 20 percent of Earth's surface. These climates lack warm summers and are typically below freezing almost year-round. A region is considered to have a polar climate if its average monthly temperature does not exceed 50°F (10°C). In a polar climate, you can expect to see ice-covered lakes throughout the year, great treeless expanses, glaciers, and a lot of snow. Vast sheets of ice cover the earth in many polar regions, meaning plants cannot survive and animal life is scarce. The air in polar climates is extremely dry, and little rain falls throughout the year. Any form of precipitation is usually snow.

Locations. The northern parts of Alaska are polar. The Arctic (North Pole) and the Antarctic (South Pole) have polar climates, with long, cold winters and cool summers. Polar conditions occur in microclimates throughout the world, such as in the high regions of the Himalayas.

Gear. If you are adventuring into the wilderness in a polar climate, you will need to be prepared with extreme cold-weather clothing made of wool or synthetic materials. No cotton! Your clothing should include a heavy jacket or parka, rain jacket, waterproof pants, waterproof mittens or gloves, wool cap, neck gaiter, boot gaiters, tall waterproof boots, wool socks, and any other items that you will need to stay warm and dry. During the summer, mosquitoes are active in some polar or near-polar regions; carry a personal bug net or hat with a net.

Health/safety. If you plan to travel to the mountains or glaciers, you should be experienced and/or be led by an experienced guide. Do not travel alone.

Before venturing into a polar climate, know how to prevent and treat hypothermia, frostbite, frostnip, and trench foot. Snow and/or ice should not be "eaten" as they require precious calories to melt and will bring your core body temperature down. If you are going to use snow to hydrate yourself, be sure to melt it first.

Polar bears are a danger, and someone in your party should be armed with a rifle that is capable of subduing a bear. Keep your distance from all wildlife, but know that they will be your primary food source should your packed food supplies run out.

Food acquisition. Natural food sources are scarce in polar climates. If you don't bring the item with you, you won't have it. On the fringe of polar climates, where the ice layer is less thick and vegetation grows, you may find plants during the summer and animals throughout the year. Food sources in this climate come from hunting seals, caribou, or small game, and from ice fishing. If you are successful at hunting, consume as much of an animal as possible, especially in a survival situation, including the internal organs such as the heart, lungs, and kidneys. However, do not eat the liver; livers of many polar animals contain toxic levels of vitamin A.

A plant known as "caribou moss" grows on the ground and rocks on the fringes of polar climates. Although caribou moss is toxic to humans in its natural form, caribou consume it. This lichen can be boiled extensively to remove its toxins, but doing so removes much of its nutrients. You can eat caribou moss safely by consuming it from the stomach of the caribou and after microorganisms in the animal's stomach have broken it down. This partially digested lichen is rich in carbohydrates, which you cannot get from eating just the meat of the caribou.

Edible berries found in polar regions include crowberries, low-bush cranberries (actually a lingonberry), blueberries, salmonberries, and cloudberries. These berries can be consumed raw or made into a treat by mixing them with sugar and milk before freezing them. *Akutaq* is a local name for this concoction packed with nutrients and calories.

Terrain concerns. Often, adventurers are drawn to the polar wilderness to climb mountains. Polar mountains are steep, jagged, rugged, and downright treacherous. You should not venture into these mountains unless you have an experienced guide or a vast amount of training as well as the proper gear. With polar mountains come high elevations, decreased oxygen, and altitude sickness. Before you head out, know the signs of acute mountain sickness (AMS), high-altitude pulmonary edema (HAPE), and high-altitude cerebral edema (HACE). If you experience symptoms of any of these conditions, descend rapidly. See chapter 7 for further details about treating altitude sickness.

In polar regions, valleys may contain rivers and lakes that are covered with snow and ice. Especially if you are transitioning into a warmer temperate climate, watch out for thin ice and exercise extreme caution if crossing any frozen water.

Ocean shoreline is also an area transitioning from a polar climate to a warmer climate. Ice and glaciers can be very unstable. Look for large cracks in the ice, and if you see them, move away quickly. Cracks are common near the edges of ice and glaciers, but they can also be found several hundred feet from the edge. If a crack breaks open, expect a long plunge into icy waters followed by a mountain of ice rolling on top of you. Watch your step!

Temperate Climates

Temperate climates experience all four seasons and great temperature variation throughout the year. The majority of the world's population lives in or near a temperate climate; therefore, most of your adventures will be in this climate as well. Temperate zones include ecosystems that are rich in life and resources, making these zones hospitable but also dangerous as adventurers must prepare for many variables.

Locations. The two types of temperate climates are maritime and continental. Maritime climates are influenced by the ocean and have more stable temperatures throughout the year. California and the United Kingdom are good examples of regions with temperate maritime climates. Farther inland, you begin to experience continental climates with warmer summers and colder winters. In the United States, the Rocky Mountains, which make up part of the Continental Divide, act as a barrier to maritime winds blowing in from the west. Popular wilderness destinations in temperate climates include areas in much of North America, Western Europe, Japan, Chile, South Africa, and South Australia.

Gear. Pack for all seasons to prepare for quick, frequent changes in weather. Even during the summer, you should bring a light jacket, a change of wool socks, and hiking boots to change into if you are wearing lighter footwear like sandals. Items that serve multiple purposes suit the climate well. For example, a rain poncho can be worn but also can be used as an emergency shelter and as a water collector. A metal water bottle can carry water and can also be used to boil and purify water, to cook food in, or as a heater if you put hot water in it, seal it tightly, and wrap it in a T-shirt or other cloth. See chapter 2 for more detailed gear recommendations.

Health/safety. Groundwater carries bacteria, especially when near human populations. Purifying your water in temperate zones is always best.

Black and brown bears, rattlesnakes, copperhead snakes, water moccasin snakes, and mountain lions are the primary predators in temperate climates. However, every animal you encounter is a wild animal and should be treated as such. Even herbivores like deer, elk, and especially moose should be respected and given a wide berth as they can easily turn aggressive.

Weather patterns change on a daily, if not an hourly, basis in temperate climates, making them one of the most difficult environments for which to prepare. Therefore, when venturing out, you should have clothing layers and a basic survival kit that will allow you to build a fire and an expedient emergency shelter.

Food acquisition. Temperate climates are full of food so long as you know what to look for and are willing to step outside of your comfort zone. Other than a few exceptions, you can eat just about anything that walks, crawls, flies, or swims in these areas. Avoid brightly colored or hairy insects, but all other insects can be eaten after cooking. Ants, termites, and their larvae are the only insects that can be safely eaten raw. Insects cook quickly over a campfire and only need a short exposure to kill any parasites they may have. You can boil insects in water for several minutes, but for flavor and texture, I prefer to lightly roast them either on a hot rock or over hot coals until they turn a slightly darker color or golden brown. Depending on the temperature of your coals, roasting an insect could take mere seconds if the coals are very hot or a minute or two. Avoid eating toads and brightly colored frogs, as their skin can have venomous glands. The armadillo can spread leprosy to humans. Mice, rats, opossum, and other large rodents that feed on waste can carry diseases such as rabies or plague, but they are not always carriers. Take great care when cleaning and cooking these animals.

Hundreds of edible plant species grow in this climate, but many poisonous plants grow as well. Importantly, you should learn your plants well, or you risk the chance of consuming a toxic or poisonous plant. As a general rule about wild berries, 80 percent of black or blue berries are edible, 50 percent of red berries are edible, and 80 percent of white berries are poisonous.

Though this general rule is a good place to start, don't play the odds. Know your berries, too!

Terrain concerns. In a temperate climate, you can expect to run into every terrain and transition zone, which isn't a bad thing. Just do your homework so you know how to prepare.

Mountains in temperate climates are far less treacherous than those in polar climates, but above 11,000 to 12,000 feet in elevation, trees do not grow. This boundary is called the timberline. If you proceed much past the timberline, the climate will likely behave more like a polar environment than a temperate one.

Water runs into valleys, bringing with it a plethora of resources. Exercise caution, as valleys—especially narrow valleys or canyons—are susceptible to flash floods. If it starts raining hard while you are in a narrow valley, seek higher ground until the rain stops and some time has passed. Keep in mind that although it might not be raining heavily where you are, a thunderous downpour may be taking place upstream. If you hear what sounds like a freight train rushing toward you, get to higher ground as quickly as possible. Don't run downstream; run up the closest hill.

Arid Climates

Arid climates, also known as deserts, are characterized by a lack of water, which limits plant growth and animal life. Plants and animals in the desert are often smaller and have unique adaptations to survive in this harsh environment. Although the desert can be hot during the day, it is often extremely cold at night.

Locations. The scope of this climate is much broader than famous deserts like the Sahara or Death Valley. Much of the southwestern United States, including popular destinations like Moab in Utah, the Grand Canyon, and Joshua Tree National Park, has an arid climate. Northwest India, South Africa, and most of Australia are also considered arid regions due to lack of precipitation.

Gear. In arid environments, dress in water-wicking undergarments and a lightweight, light-colored, loose-fitting cotton mid layer to keep you cool and to keep the sun off your skin. Pack a hair/beard comb to remove cactus thorns from your skin. Pack warm layers for the evenings and for sleeping, as the temperature in the desert drops sharply after sunset.

Health/safety. The key to surviving an arid climate is getting out of the direct sun then finding water. The best way to do both is to locate a shaded canyon or valley.

You not only can find shelter from the sun in canyons but also dry riverbeds or washes that may have water below the earth. The best time to find water is during the early morning when condensation collects on rocks and vegetation. Look for shaded areas near boulders or rock formations that get little sun throughout the day and dig down to see if the soil or sand is moist. Boulders in desert canyons may also have indentations or bowls in the top where water collects.

Paying attention to the vegetation will also help you find water. If you spot large trees like cottonwood or willow or other green trees, you'll find water in that location. The possibility of drinking water from a cactus is a myth. The water is not only difficult to access but also is high in acids, which will make you sick. If you do find water, boil it whenever possible. See chapter 4 for best practices for purifying water.

If you cannot find water, your best and only survival tactic is to get out of the desert. Don't stay put. Only travel in the evenings and early mornings when the sun is not out. Before the sun comes up, find a shaded area and rest during the day to conserve your energy and water.

Remember that the desert gets very cold at night, and because your body has adapted to the heat of the day, the night cold is amplified, which means finding a shelter and making a fire is very important. Look for caves or boulders that block wind and sun and can protect you from animals. Don't be afraid to build a rock barrier to keep the animals and elements away. Gather dried grasses, shrubs, and dead cactus to use for your fire.

Rattlesnakes and scorpions run rampant in many arid climates. Scorpions burrow under rocks, debris piles, and old wood lying on the ground. Because scorpions feed on insects, beware of dark places where other insects may reside. Take great care when flipping over rocks or gathering firewood. Rattlesnakes cannot regulate their body temperature. If you feel warm and comfortable in the sun, then rattlesnakes will be out enjoying the sun, too. If you are seeking shade, rattlesnakes are, too. Beware of tall grasses, dark holes, and rock ledges, where snakes may go to get out of the direct sun.

Food acquisition. As you are on the lookout for snakes and scorpions, remember that they are great to eat. Take extra care when hunting them, using a forked stick to pin a rattlesnake's head to the ground or a container to capture scorpions. Other animals don't come out during the day, so be sure to set up plenty of traps around your camp to catch them at night when the weather is cooler.

Terrain concerns. Arid mountains do not have an overabundance of water and lack cover from the sun. Although resources may be found in the mountains, if you are unable to get out of the sun, they are not worth the amount of water that you will expend getting to them.

Valleys and canyons in arid climates can be your friends as they may provide water collection points, shade, and other resources. However, during a rainstorm, they are your enemy as they are very susceptible to flash floods and mudflows. Flood risks can shift dramatically because watersheds are unstable, so do not rely on historical flood data to guide your actions. Be wary when dark clouds roll in over you or upstream from you.

All arid terrains include the risk of a haboob or severe sandstorm. Take great caution to protect your eyes, nose, and mouth during these storms as blowing sand and clay will damage your eyes and may cause severe respiratory distress. A shemagh or large cotton scarf is widely used in desert climates to protect the head and face.

Tropical and Subtropical Climates

When contemplating a wilderness adventure in a tropical or subtropical climate, I find it helpful to think of regions with such a climate as having two seasons: a wet season and a dry season with some rain. Having spent several weeks in the jungles of Costa Rica, I typically relate a tropical climate with a jungle, which is not always the case; the savanna is also considered tropical and gets far less rain.

The jungle is a beautiful yet dangerous place. Birds, monkeys, reptiles, frogs, wild pigs, and even large cats are everywhere you look. Bullet ants, large tarantulas, and other creepy crawlers exist in huge numbers. Once the sun starts to descend in the late afternoon, the jungle quickly gets dark due to the heavy canopy overhead.

Locations. The only place in the United States that is truly tropical is Hawaii. The southernmost parts of the United States, including Southern California, southern Florida, and southern Texas, are subtropical regions. Around the world, popular tropical and subtropical adventure destinations include Costa Rica, the Amazon basin, Northern Australia, and much of Oceania.

Gear. When in doubt, carry the gear that the locals carry. When I was in Costa Rica, our local guide carried a well-used machete for bushwhacking, along with a mill file to keep it sharp. He also carried a large sack of rice, a large water bottle, a sturdy rain poncho, a BIC lighter, and a bicycle inner tube cut into strips so that he could easily start a fire. I would also recommend bug spray, a hammock sleep system with a durable under-layer or sleeping pad and a bug net to ward off mosquitoes, a virus-grade water filter, ear plugs (tropical nightlife is loud), and durable rain gear.

Health/safety. Waterborne pathogens are a great concern in tropical environments. Cholera, dysentery, *Cryptosporidium*, and giardia infection are spread by water contamination and can cause symptoms like cramps, fever, vomiting, and diarrhea, which can lead to severe dehydration and even death. Remember, too, that severe sunburns are very danger-ous. Wear clothing to protect yourself from overexposure to the sun.

Other concerns are hiking on unmarked lava trails, coco-nuts falling from trees, a variety of venomous snakes, floods, hurricanes, droughts, bullet ants, howler monkeys or other primates, wild boars, cougars, or other local wildlife. When tra-versing through tropical environments, carefully watch what is on the ground beneath you and what is hanging in the trees above you.

Food acquisition. Food sources abound in tropical environ-ments, including freshwater shrimp, all the insects you can eat, coconuts, plantains, and heart of palm.

The easiest palm trees to obtain heart of palm from have a thin spread of leaves at the top of the tree, accompanied by a large green trunk section (growing bud) just beneath the leaves, and a root system that fans out at the base of the tree but aboveground. These trees closely resemble a large witch's broom that has been jammed into the ground with the brush portion just barely exposed. Don't confuse this tree with the "walking palm," which has roots that stick out several feet aboveground.

To acquire freshwater shrimp, look for clumps of fallen leaves in slow-moving streams. Carefully wade up to the clump of leaves that have fallen into the water, then quickly grab as many of the leaves as you can and throw the bundle of leaves onto the shoreline. Pick through the leaves you cast ashore to see if you were lucky enough to have snagged some shrimp. If you brought rice with you, build a bamboo stove and add rice, heart of palm, shrimp, and water to the inside of the stove. Start a fire, and in 20 minutes, you will have an amazing and nutrient-rich meal.

Terrain concerns. Mountains and valleys of tropical climates are resource-rich, especially in forested environments. However, steep slopes are usually unstable and difficult to traverse. Take great care with your footing when descending or ascending these slopes.

Tropical and subtropical islands and shorelines are subject to hazards such as hurricanes, earthquakes, and tidal waves. Keep an eye on the sky and watch the water on the horizon.

ADVENTURE STORIES: UNEXPECTED WEATHER

My home state of Colorado, like many places around the world, has diverse climates and terrains with weather patterns that change suddenly. This environment has taught me the importance of being well-prepared and adaptable. I have been trapped in an unexpected springtime blizzard that dropped four feet of snow overnight. On another trip, I was caught in a torrential downpour at dusk, which washed away the tent and soaked my partner and me to the core; only moments earlier, the sun was out. With the fast-dropping temperatures, the night would have been very unpleasant if we hadn't been physically and mentally prepared.

These potentially hazardous experiences became training opportunities as I assessed the situation and made educated decisions about what to do without allowing ego to get in the way. During the spring blizzard, we constructed a crude shelter and hunkered down. In the intense rainstorm, we dried off next to a hot fire, packed up our wet gear, and hiked out under the cover of night to return to our planned adventure another day.

CHAPTER FOUR

BACK TO BASICS

Bushcrafting is the ability to recognize the useful natural resources around you and the art of leveraging those resources to create tools. Although bushcrafting is considered a hobby by many, the skills involved in bushcrafting are very useful for wilderness survival should you find yourself without modern tools. With proper training and practice, you can create everything you need from the natural environment. Our ancestors did so for many lifetimes before modern technology came into play. Unfortunately, many of these skills have been forgotten through the years. This chapter will help you recover these lost skills.

Fire

Creating and maintaining a sustainable fire is one of the most valuable survival skills. Some experts advocate for using a magnifying glass or flint and steel to start fires, but these are not practical approaches. Both techniques require that you carry unlikely items—like a magnifying glass, flint, and preprepared char cloth. Furthermore, a magnifying glass only works when the sun is out. The techniques listed here are more practical and reliable, and can be used in almost any environment.

Setting a Fire Lay

Uses. Any time you need to start a fire, setting a fire lay is your first and most important step. Take the time to set your lay right the first time.

Materials. If you do not carry tinder in your kit, gather dry tinder throughout the day and store it in your pack. Tinder is material that can easily be set on fire with little more than a spark, such as fine grasses, shredded cottonwood bark, or cotton balls and petroleum jelly. Kindling is larger flammable material and can be as thin as wire or as thick as your wrist. Common kindling materials are pine needles, thick pieces of cottonwood bark, or dry twigs from any tree.

Time and effort. Setting your lay should take you 5 to 15 minutes. Some walking and extensive foraging in poor weather conditions may be required, but the time you spend looking for proper materials is well worth the trouble.

Instructions

Select a fire lay that works best for your materials.

1. Create a tinder bundle that is at least the size of your head. Materials like grasses and barks in their natural form are not optimal tinder. Process your tinder materials into smaller hair-like fibers by vigorously rolling them between your hands and twisting, bending, and crushing them. Don't snap the material in half, as you want your tinder fibers to be long, thin, and frayed.

2. Once your raw tinder materials are worked into thin strands, shape them into a bird's nest. The next step is to ready your kindling.

3. Sort your kindling into three different piles by size. For the best results, larger kindling should be split or made into feathersticks to expose dry areas and create more surface area. Create feathersticks by running your knife blade down a long piece of wood, at a shallow angle, to shave curls into the wood. The goal is to create thin slices that remain attached to the main piece of wood.

4. Once your tinder and kindling are processed, you can build your fire lay. You can either build your fire lay with the kindling first, leaving room for the burning tinder to be inserted inside the lay after the tinder is lit, or you can light your tinder first and build your lay around it.

Simple fire lays are the teepee, log cabin, lean-to, and A-frame. Experiment to see which method you prefer. No matter which fire lay you choose, don't use too much wood at first; a fire needs both fuel (wood) and oxygen to burn.

Starting a Fire with Fatwood

Uses. If you cannot find dry wood and find yourself in a pine forest, you can use fatwood (also called lighter wood) to start a fire. Pine is full of sap and resins, which are highly flammable. When a pine tree is damaged, resins flow to the area of the tree that is damaged to try to heal itself. Or when the tree dies, all of the resins flow down into the base of the trunk. The resins impregnate the wood in these areas, making it dense, waterproof, and flammable.

Materials. Dead pine branches, pine stumps, or pine logs. Fatwood can only be found in pine trees.

Time and effort. Five to 15 minutes. The hardest part of building a fire with fatwood is finding the fatwood and processing it down into a usable material.

Fatwood is a rich golden color and smells strongly of pine.

Instructions

1. Locate a dead pine tree or a dead branch on a living pine tree. You will not find fatwood by cutting down living trees.

2. Once you have located a dead branch, cut it off next to the main trunk. Pine wood is typically white or light in color. If the section that you cut off is a rich caramel color and has the heavy scent of Pine-Sol, it is probably fatwood. If you have located a tree stump, the outside portions of the stump may be rotted and crumbling; hack away the outer portions until you find an unusually dense and solid inner core. You may have to dig underground into the root system.

3. Using your knife, remove small, dust-like shavings from the fatwood. Removing the shavings will take effort as the wood is dense.

4. Once you have a processed pile of fatwood dust, place the pile in your fire lay. Only use what you need and place the rest in your survival kit.

Because of the resins in the wood, fatwood burns for an extended time and can be used as both tinder and kindling. Fatwood readily takes a spark from a ferrocerium rod or lighter.

Starting a Fire with a Ferrocerium Rod

Uses. A ferrocerium rod means that you will have the ability to start a fire whenever you need one, as long as you have fire-making materials. Do not confuse a ferro rod with flint and steel. Some people use these names interchangeably, but they are not the same thing.

Materials. You will need a ferrocerium rod and a hard, rigid striker like your knife. Use the back spine of your knife rather than the blade to avoid damaging it. Flint rocks, quartz rocks, or sea-shells can also be used as strikers.

Time and effort. Starting a fire with a ferro rod should only take one minute. Once you figure out the proper technique, your effort will be minimal. If you aren't seeing sparks, change what you are doing until you get the desired results.

Starting a fire with a ferrocerium rod.

Instructions

1. Gather your fire-making material first. Process your tinder and kindling, and set your lay.

2. New ferro rods come with a layer of paint on them. This paint helps keep them from rusting and deteriorating in humid climates. Scrape off the paint in a small area before using your rod for the first time.

3. Grasp your striker firmly in your main hand while holding the end of the ferro rod in your off hand.

4. Lock the elbow of your main hand, making your arm rigid. Your main, or striker, hand should remain stationary near your tinder bundle. The other hand holding the ferro rod is the hand that moves, focusing the sparks in the immediate area of your tinder bundle.

5. With your main hand locked at the elbow and wrist, place the top edge of the ferro rod against the bottom edge of your striker, and firmly press them together. Without moving your main hand, while still applying as much pressure as you can, quickly pull your off hand backward, scraping the edge of the ferro rod along the edge of your striker. You will see a shower of sparks.

6. Repeat step 5 until your tinder pile ignites. If the tinder pile does not ignite after a few tries, fluff it up.

Starting a Bow Drill Friction Fire

Uses. Always be prepared with the proper gear. But should you lose all your gear, you can still get a fire going with natural materials by making a bow drill friction fire. The bow drill lets you create enough friction to make a hot coal with which to ignite a fire.

Materials. In order to start a friction fire with a bow drill, you will need the following.

- **Bow.** Use a tree branch of arm's length and about one inch in diameter, with a slight curve and limited flexibility. Your branch should be light but strong, and one end should fit comfortably in your hand, like you are holding a long knife.

- **Bow string.** Your bow string will be a length of paracord, shoelace, or natural cordage that is 12 to 18 inches longer than your bow. String the cord loosely from one end of your bow to the other.

- **Drill.** To form the drill, whittle a 10- to 18-inch straight piece of dry wood into the shape of a sharpened pencil (with one blunt end and one sharp end) about the diameter of your little finger.

- **Fireboard.** Both your drill and your fireboard must be wood that has been exposed to the elements for a long period of time and lacks any moisture, saps, or resins. This commonly includes cottonwood, cedar, aspen, willow, juniper, and poplar. Pine will work, too, but the wood must not have any sap or resin in it. The fireboard should be a 10- to 12-inch wooden plank, approximately 3 inches wide and ½ to ¾ inch thick.

- **Bearing block.** Your bearing block is a rock, bone, or whittled piece of hard wood that has a divot in it and can fit comfortably in your hand.

- **Ember pan.** An ember pan is a small, thin piece of wood, a leaf, or a piece of leather used to catch and hold the hot ember. For the best results, your ember pan should be flexible but not too thin.

- **Bird's nest.** Gather enough dry fibrous material to create a bundle roughly the size of a basketball. From this mass of fibrous material, pull out a large handful and create a bird's nest that fits in two hands. Process the material down by vigorously rolling it in your hands, crushing it, or shredding it so that it is as fine as possible but still in long strips. Make this processed nest look something like a loose ball of long hair. Using half of the other material you gathered, create a second, larger bird's nest and place it around the processed bird's nest to make one large bundle of material. Everything you have left over goes in or near your fire lay to be used later.

Time and effort. On a scale from 1 to 10, for a beginner, creating a bow drill is a level 10 effort and may take more than four hours. The process gets far easier the more you practice. An expert can complete this activity in 30 minutes.

Instructions

Before you start the following steps, be sure you have gathered enough small tinder and kindling so that you can build a sustainable fire once you create an ember. The instructions here are for a right-handed person; change your stance accordingly if you are left-handed.

1. Carve a divot in your fireboard just big enough for the blunt end of your drill to seat in. The edge of the drill should sit ½ inch to ¾ inch from the edge of your fireboard.

2. Burn in your hole. Twist your drill into your bow string so that the blunt end is facing down when you hold the bow horizontally. Place the fireboard on the ground with your left foot on the board, near the divot, and kneel down so that your right knee is on the ground, positioned in line with your left foot.

3. Seat your drill into the indentation you just carved; place your bearing block on the pointy end of the drill. Press your left hand against your leg so that your wrist is snug against your

left shin. With your left hand firmly grasping the bearing block and your right hand firmly grasping the back end of the bow, begin to saw slowly while putting downward pressure on the bearing block and drill.

4. Once you find a rhythm, pick up speed. In about 20 seconds, you should see smoke pouring out between your drill and fireboard. Keep going until you create a smooth divot in the fireboard that is about ⅛ inch deep. You have now burned in an area for your drill to seat nicely into the fireboard.

5. Carve your notch. On the side of the divot you just created, carve a triangular notch. The notch should reach almost to the middle of the circular divot, but not quite. Imagine you are cutting out a one-eighth piece of pie from the circle, but stop just shy of the middle. The notch should go clear through the fireboard, but when viewing the fireboard from the side, the notch should be in the shape of a pyramid.

6. Repeat steps 2–4, but this time, place the ember pan beneath the fireboard, under the notch, so that the pan catches any dust you create. As you saw or "bow," the notch will fill up with dust. Saw slowly at first, just fast enough to generate heat, friction, and dust. If you are doing this correctly, you should see smoke in about 15 seconds. The dust should be dark brown or black. If it

isn't, then pick up the speed and apply a little more pressure.

Dust will begin to pile up on the ember pan. Once the dust pile fills the notch, increase your speed and pressure, making sure not to move so quickly that you lose control. You will get tired.

After 45 seconds or 1 minute, smoke should billow from the notch. Once you think you have a coal, go for another 10 seconds with increased speed and pressure but maintain control. Once you are ready to stop, continue for five more seconds just to be sure that you have created a sufficient coal.

7. Relax! Don't make any fast movements. If you created a coal, you have 10 to 15 minutes to get to the next step. Do not remove your foot from the board yet. Moving smoothly and steadily, remove your drill and bow, and place them on the ground near you. Firmly place your fingers on the fireboard, and only then remove your foot to avoid jarring the board and losing your ember.

Leaving your fingers in place, grasp your drill and gently tap the fireboard with it to loosen the ember from the notch. While tapping, slowly roll the board back and away from the ember pan. If the dust sticks to the board, tap it just a little bit harder with the drill. Once the dust breaks free, set the fireboard and drill to the side. You should be left with a small pile of smoldering dust on your ember pan.

8. Fan your ember. You have a hot ember; now you need to let it grow and give it oxygen to make it hotter and bigger. With your hand, gently fan the smoking pile of dust to help the ember spread. *Don't blow on it with your mouth*, as you may blow too hard and the moisture in your breath can do more harm than good. Fan the ember until it becomes red hot. Once the ember is red hot, stop fanning and give it 15 seconds to set up a little more.

9. Transfer your ember to the center of your bird's nest. Gently pick up your ember pan in one hand and your full bird's nest in the other. Fold the nest into the ember pan and gently transfer the ember. Tap the bottom of the ember pan to break free the hot ember, then set the ember pan to the side. Now gently fold the nest around the ember so that you can't see it and begin to blow. Blow gently at first, like you are blowing seeds off a dandelion. A little smoke, a little breath. The more smoke you see, the harder you should blow. Don't be afraid to move the bundle around in your hands to disperse the heat and oxygen. As long as you see smoke, keep blowing. If you don't see smoke, gently open the nest to see if your ember went out. If it did, start over. Don't open the nest too often; each time you

do, you lose progress if the ember is in fact still burning.

If the smoke is blowing into your face, turn your entire body so the smoke blows away from you, and hold the nest slightly above your face so that the smoke moves up and away. If you see the smoke change from a wispy white to a thick yellowish color, the nest is ready to ignite. Blow harder, but watch your eyebrows.

10. Transfer your nest to your fire lay. Slowly add the rest of the plant material that you previously gathered, and make sure your fire does not go out. Be careful not to put too much material on the fire too fast.

Water

Water is a vital resource. In general, a human can survive for three to five days without water, although in extreme situations, you will not want to go more than one day without water. In a survival situation, you should be constantly searching for water if it is not readily available in the form of a stream or lake. Once you have found water, you must collect and purify it.

Locating Water

Water can be found anywhere. Scan your environment for holes, crevices, and low points where water may collect. The early morning is the best time to find and collect morning dew from plants.

If you see an unusual amount of green vegetation or large trees when all the other plant life is smaller, water is probably nearby. If the ground is covered in thick grass but is also soft and squishy under your feet, water may be nearby, too.

Although water tends to flow downhill and be in lower shaded areas, you can find water on hilltops or even on the top of a mountain if you find a collection point. In winter, melt ice or snow.

Thoroughly search an area for collecting points before moving on to a new area. You may need to dig a hole or multiple holes, but do not expend too much energy digging very deep. Don't stop once you find one resource or method. Combine digging holes with looking in or on plants. Follow animal trails if you find them; animals need water, too, and will travel the same path to their favorite watering hole.

Capturing Water

With a large water source like a stream, large puddle, or lake, you can easily gather water into a container. However, should the water be in the form of morning dew or underground, capturing it will take some work.

Morning dew or very shallow collection points. Using a cotton scarf, T-shirt, or clean sock, sop up the water until you have absorbed enough to wring out into a container. If your terrain has tall grass, collect dew by tying a cloth around your lower leg and walking through the grass.

Ice and snow. In a survival scenario, eating ice and snow is not safe, as it will cool down your core body temperature and consume much-needed calories. Melt snow before putting it in your body. Gather a large mass of snow in a scarf or T-shirt and hang it next to your fire, placing a container beneath it to catch the dripping water. You can also place smaller amounts of ice and snow in a metal container and set the container next to your fire to melt.

Seep well. If you suspect water is underground, dig a hole roughly 18 inches deep. If water is present, it will slowly start to fill up the hole. This process might take minutes or hours, depending on water levels. Drinking straight from a seep well is not safe, as the water may contain bacteria or viruses.

Purifying Water

Filter and boil. Outside of a modern water purifier, the most practical way to make your water safer to drink is to boil it. The CDC states that boiling your water for three minutes will make it safe to drink. If your water is murky, I recommend boiling it for 10 minutes. Boiling water does not remove sediment or organic materials, so you may want to filter it first to remove unwanted floaties and undesirable tastes and smells.

To filter your water, simply pass it through a scarf to remove sediment. You can set up a more complex water filter using grass, pebbles, sand, and crushed charcoal from a fire. Sand and grass will remove sediment whereas charcoal will bind to smaller particles, making your water taste and smell better. This process will filter your water only; your water will not be purified until it is boiled.

Rock boiling. If you do not have a container to hold water or a device to purify it, you will need to create one by carving wood or by burning out the center of a log using a hot coal from your fire.

Once you have created a container, heat rocks in your fire. Select rocks that are small enough to easily fit in your container but large enough that you can fish them out of the fire with sticks or a small shovel. Do not use river rocks or dense glassy rocks such as quartz, shale, or flint as they can explode when heated.

Once your rocks are hot, fill your container with water, pull the hot rocks from the fire, and gently place them into your water-filled container. Try not to remove any ash from the rocks before placing them in the water. Remove the rocks as they cool, and add new hot rocks to the water until it boils for three minutes. Your water is now safer to drink.

Create a bowl by burning out the center of a log with a hot coal.

Treating with chemicals. Use this method sparingly because an improper mixture of chemicals or their overuse can kill the good bacteria in your stomach. If you use water purification tablets, follow the package instructions.

Primitive Shelters

Building an effective shelter that is windproof and water-proof takes time and energy. If you have a premade (natural or man-made) shelter available, use it. If not, use the resources around you. In a survival situation, your shelter should be small and use just enough resources to protect you from the elements, at least for the first night. Once you have determined you will need to stay for more than one night and have procured food and water, you can construct a larger, more comfortable shelter.

If you do not have shelter and cannot find a cave or rock overhang, the following are some easy-to-build alternatives. A folding handsaw and rope will make shelter building easier.

Lean-to. A lean-to is a single ridge pole, along with rib poles that extend at an angle from the ridge pole to the ground. If your ridge pole is lower to the ground, you will have an easier time heating your shelter and you will use fewer resources to build it. However, a lower shelter is also less comfortable to be inside of. If you will be in one place for an extended period of time, make your lean-to bigger after the first night.

When you are building your lean-to, pay attention to how you place your rib poles. If you have a tarp, the rib poles can be spaced several inches apart. If you don't, the rib poles need to be placed against one another to fill all the gaps.

Basic lean-to structure.

Alternate poles (or trees), with every other tree being laid in upside down. This method will allow the bottom and the top of the roof to be the same width and will fill out the ridge pole appropriately.

Once the structure is built, heap leaves on top of the shelter to make it waterproof. Fill the inside of the shelter with dry leaves so that you do not lose body heat through contact with the cold ground.

If you need additional warmth, you can add a fire pit in front of your structure, a wall on the opposite side of the fire pit to reflect the heat, or side porches for gear, pets, or other people.

A-frame. An A-frame shelter is also known as a "jungle hooch." This shelter is great when you need to be off the ground, either in wet or snow-covered environments. This shelter requires a considerable amount of rope, cordage, or vines to build. If you do not have a tarp, you will have to fashion a roof out of natural materials.

To build this shelter, collect four sturdy support legs. These legs should be stout and at least a foot taller than you. Next, collect the horizontal support for the "A." This part should also be a stout section of tree. Lash these sections together to create two separate structures that are in the shape of an "A" with the top of the "A" extended to make a small "X." Place the "A's" upright and place a ridge pole on the tops of the "A's" where the "X's" were created. The ridge pole should be at least a foot longer than you are tall.

Cut smaller branches to form your bed, and place them between the two horizontal supports of the "A's." For maximum comfort, the trees forming your bed platform should be just thick enough to hold your weight with some bend or spring to them. Lash the bed rails to the frame, then fill the platform with leaves. If you have a tarp, place it over the top to keep you dry.

Basic A-frame structure.

Platform bed. In some environments, you may need to get off the ground, away from creepy crawlies, standing water, or flash floods. If you are not able to build an A-frame, a crude platform bed is your best option.

To build a platform bed, find a few trees that are growing relatively close together in a triangular formation. The trees should have large branches protruding at approximately the same height. If the trees don't have branches, you can lash support beams directly to the tree, but you will need some sort of cordage. If no suitable trees are available, hammer posts into the ground.

Attach horizontal beams to your trees or posts, then place smaller branches that will support your weight on these beams to form a platform. If you do not have cordage, you will need to find trees that have well-placed branches that allow you to

wedge your support beams where you need them. If you can find leaves, cover the platform for comfort. If you are in an environment with a wet, muddy ground, place a thick layer of mud on the end of the structure where your feet will go. This layer of mud should be four to six inches thick and can be used as a small fire pit. Be sure to apply enough mud over every piece of wood that the flames might hit.

Snow cave. Be cautious when building snow caves. They should be used as a last resort, when your terrain has a lot of snow, no trees, and you need to get out of the wind. If your snow cave is not built properly, you risk carbon dioxide

poisoning or suffocation. And, if you are unable to put a barrier between yourself and the snow, you risk hypothermia and severe frostbite. Snow caves are difficult to build without tools. If you are headed into the backcountry during the winter, carry a packable snow shovel.

The proper design of a snow cave is somewhat complex. First, you will need to find a safe place to build, with deep enough snow and away from avalanche zones. The entry to your shelter should be as low on the structure as possible. Warm air rises, so a door at the top of the shelter constantly loses any heat you may create.

A good snow shelter should have three levels. The lowest level, nearest the door, is the cold well, where the coolest air settles. The next level is your working bench, and the top level is your sleeping area. Dig out or poke a small hole in the ceiling to promote air circulation. Never sleep or sit for extended periods directly on the snow. Line the floor of your working bench and sleeping area with blankets, leaves, or pine boughs.

Ropes, Lines, and Knots

Every knot has a purpose, but this book cannot cover them all. This section opens with a series of common scenarios—like lashing a pole to a tree to build a shelter or creating a noose for a trap—and instructions for applying the knots you'd likely need in those instances. At the end of this chapter (page 89) are step-by-step illustrations for all the knots mentioned in the scenarios.

Whatever your situation, be sure you are using the proper rope for the job. For instance, never climb or rappel using rope that is not made for the task.

Building Shelter: Securely Lashing a Ridge Pole to a Tree or Post

Knots. Clove hitch with frapping and a square knot.

Materials. For a rail and a post with diameters of three to four inches, you will need 12 to 16 feet of paracord or other rope.

Instructions

1. Start by tying a clove hitch around the horizontal rail, as close to the vertical post as possible. Position the knot so that the long end will lay across the top of the rail. Leave four inches of cordage on the short end of the rope. You will use this section to tie off in the end.

2. Once the rope is attached to the rail, form an "X" with the rope on the back side of the post by wrapping the rope over, around, and under your post and rail.

3. Repeat step 2 until you have wrapped around the post two or three times. When finished, you should have about two feet of cordage left on the long end plus the four-inch tail on the first side.

4. Look between the rail and post, and you will see that the lashing has four points of contact. You will use frapping wraps around the four points and squeeze them together. To do so, wrap the remaining two feet of cordage in between the post and rail to touch these four points and pull very hard. Frap as many times as you can, leaving enough tail to tie into the original four-inch tail (using a square knot). The use of a square knot on the end is important because this type of knot is easy to untie when it's time to dismantle the shelter and move on.

Securing an Item to a Post with an Easy Release Knot

Use this knot when you need to secure something to a post but want to be able to easily untie it later. This knot can be tied while wearing heavy gloves. It should not be used to tie heavy overhead loads due to the ease of its release. I use this knot as my first knot when securing tarp shelters to a tree.

Knots. Siberian hitch.

Materials. Any length of rope.

Instructions

1. Tie one end of your rope around the tarp or other item that you want to secure.

2. Cradle the rope in the palm of your hand, and wrap the working end of the rope around a tree or post.

3. Once your rope is wrapped around the tree, loosely wrap the working end around your fingers once and tightly pinch the two ends of the rope with your thumb and forefinger, using the hand that the rope is not wrapped around.

4. With the rope wrapped around your fingers, slide the wrapped hand under the secured end that is cradled in the same hand and twist your hand over.

5. Reach over the secured end and grab the center of the short tail and pull it partially through the loop that is around your fingers.

6. While holding the loop you just created, pull on the end that is secured to the main object and pull tight to the post.

7. If you wish to make the knot difficult to untie, place a stick or toggle inside of the loop. When you wish to release the knot, simply remove the toggle and pull the tail end.

Securing Cordage to a Bow for Your Bow Drill Set

To tie your cordage to your bow drill for a bow drill friction fire, use a combination of an arbor knot and a clove hitch. This combination knot is a slip knot that can also be used to compress and tie down sleeping bags, bed rolls, blankets, or other items you may need to secure to your backpack.

Knots. Arbor knot (aka Canadian jam knot) and clove hitch.

Materials. Paracord or shoelace roughly 18 inches longer than the bow used for your bow drill set.

Instructions

1. Begin by tying an arbor knot around the thin end of your bow. The tail or excess should be minimal. You may need to create a small notch in your bow so that your knot doesn't slip down the stick.

2. Loosely string the bow, and at the opposite end, tie a clove hitch to secure the rope to the end of the bow that you will hold in your hand. Either wrap any excess string around the end of the bow or cut it off. I prefer to wrap it so that I am not wasting rope. The clove hitch is useful for this setup because your paracord will

eventually stretch slightly, requiring you to untie and tighten the string. The clove hitch is easy to untie.

3. Once the rope is secured to your bow, twist the drill into the bow line. The drill should be tight and pop into place. You should not be able to easily slide the drill on the rope; if you can, undo the clove hitch and tie the bow line tighter.

Tying a Noose to Create a Locking Trapper's Knot

In a survival situation, you may need to catch your food using a snare trap. The following method will help keep your dinner from getting away.

Knots. Cow hitch (aka lark's head), poacher's knot, arbor knot, and bowline knot.

Materials. Paracord, shoelace, or bank line. The length will depend on the size of your trap.

Instructions

1. Using a bowline knot, tightly secure your rope to your spring pole.

2. About 12 inches from the working end, create a poacher's knot with a long tail. After creating your loop, you should be left with about 12 inches of rope to tie to your toggle using an arbor knot.

3. With a separate section of rope, you will now create your trapper's noose. One end will be the noose, created with the lark's head knot; the other end will tie into your poacher's knot. To complete the lark's head for the trapper's noose, you will need enough rope so that you can place the noose where you need it on a path or over an animal's den. To make the noose, make a bight (a slack part or loop) in your rope, which will be your noose loop.

4. Tie the working end back upon itself using a lark's head knot. This step will create a slip knot that will get tighter around your prey and won't loosen as the animal struggles.

5. Attach this section of rope to the loop that you previously tied and set your trap.

Building a Tripod, Quadpod, or Raft

You can use this lashing with three or four legs depending on the structure you wish to build. Three legs will work for a simple cooking rack or water-filtration station, whereas four legs can be used to make a larger platform. Furthermore, you can continue adding "legs," and use this lashing style to build a raft or solid platform by lashing both ends of the legs together rather than just one.

Knots. Lashing knot and clove hitch.

Materials. Paracord, bank line, other type of rope, or vines. For a small tripod, you will need three to four feet of cordage.

Instructions

1. Begin by laying your legs or poles on the ground side by side. You will have three legs if you are building a tripod, four for a quadpod, and more if you are building a raft.

2. Tie a clove hitch around the first pole.

3. Wrap at least three racking turns around the poles, weaving in and out between each pole.

4. With the working end, make at least two frapping turns in the gaps between each pole, leaving enough rope to finish off with another clove hitch.

5. Stand the structure up and cross the outside poles to form a tripod or spread out the poles evenly to form a quadpod.

6. If building a raft, repeat steps 2–4 on the other end of the poles.

7. Horizontal rails can be added to a tripod or quadpod to make the structure sturdier or to add a rack to the center of the structure.

8. Follow the steps for securely lashing a ridge pole to a tree or post to tie in horizontal rails.

ESSENTIAL KNOTS

Clove hitch

Square knot

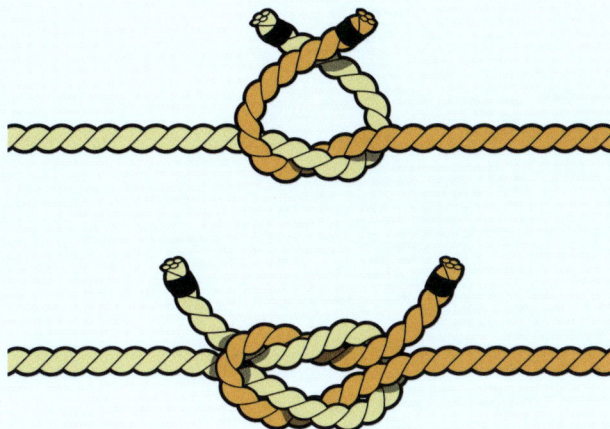

Lashing knot

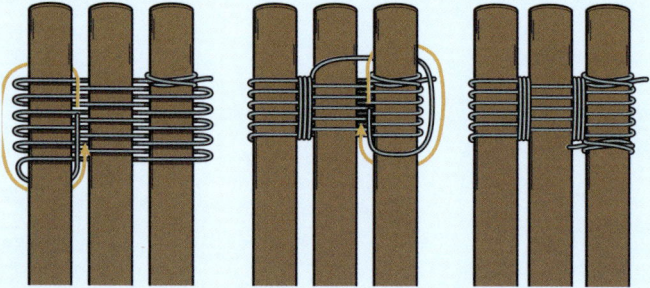

Siberian hitch (Evenk hitch)

Arbor knot (Canadian jam knot)

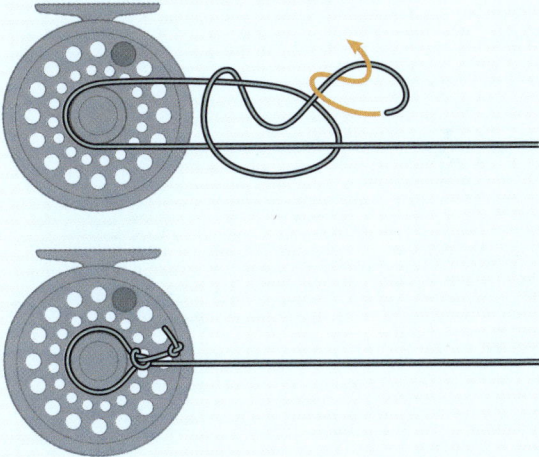

Bowline knot

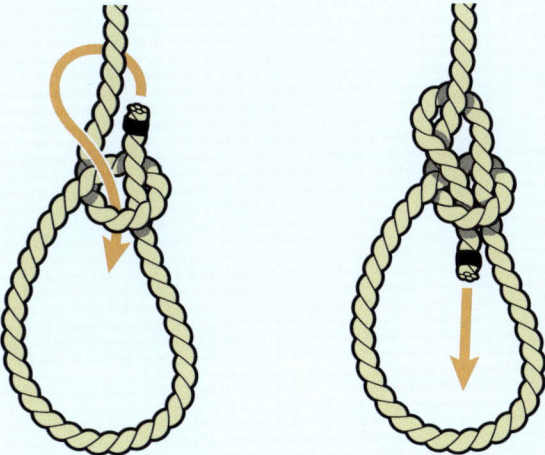

Poacher's knot

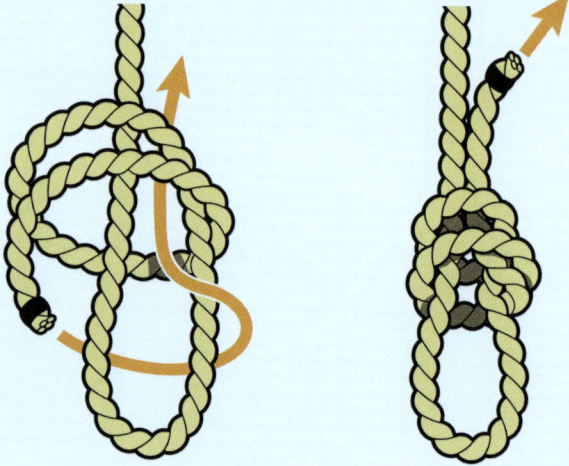

Cow hitch (lark's head)

CHAPTER FIVE

LIVING OFF THE LAND

Whether you're in the wilderness for a short overnight hike or testing your skills on an extended adventure, you'll need to master some basic skills to live off the land. Foraging for food and creating tools using natural resources has become an all but lost art. In this chapter, I hope to inspire you to continue learning about all that can be found and utilized in the natural environment.

Bird and Small Animal Traps

Hunting and trapping are highly regulated. Know your local laws before you attempt either. Hunting—actively pursuing an animal with a projectile weapon—can be rewarding but takes a lot of energy, so trapping is a better alternative for procuring food for survival. If you opt to hunt, do so in the early morning and just before sundown.

When trapping, set and check your traps during the day; animals will most likely be trapped at night. Do not take setting traps lightly. Traps are indiscriminate and will harm anything that triggers them, including domestic and endangered animals as well as humans.

Two main types of traps are the **passive trap**, a snare wire or pit with no moving parts, and an **active trap** like a spring pole or counterweight, which has moving parts.

Most active traps consist of a support structure, a trigger or bait stick, a toggle, and a killing device. The support structure holds everything in place, the toggle moves in some direction to activate the killing device, and the trigger stick keeps the toggle from moving until it's supposed to move. The following section outlines five trap types for different environments and prey.

TRAP TIPS

- Trapping is a numbers game. If you are trapping food to survive, build as many traps as you can and set new traps every day until you are constantly catching prey.
- Build a variety of traps to find out what works best. If a trap stops working, change it up or move traps around.
- Check your traps often. You will be competing with scavengers, so check your traps with caution. Check them first thing every morning and every night before the sun goes down.
- Trapping takes practice. The first time you build and set a trap will take a considerable amount of time. You'll get better; don't give up.
- Mark or map your traps so that you can easily find them.
- Bait your traps accordingly. Pay attention to what animals are eating and use their food as bait. Man-made bait, such as peanut butter, is not always your best option.
- Use entrails as bait for your next trap. Entrails will attract birds, larger scavengers, or predators (which are edible, too), and most rodents are cannibalistic and omnivorous.

- Set your traps to the side of game trails. Setting your traps directly on a large game trail is usually not productive.
- Set your traps near water sources, especially on small trails that lead to water sources.
- Take a smoke bath before setting or checking your traps to mask your human scent. Let newly built traps sit in smoke or in cool ash before you set them. Handle them as little as possible.
- Disturb the area around the traps as little as possible. Try not to get your odor on everything.
- Dismantle any traps before moving on, and take with you what you can reasonably carry.

Wire Snare Trap

Uses. The wire snare trap is a snare loop anchored to a structure. These traps work well for predictable animals like squirrels and rabbits.

Materials. These traps are best built with wire or cable wire, but paracord or natural cordage can be used as well. The larger the animal you intend to trap, the longer the wire should be. Two feet of wire works well for rabbits. Use a sturdy branch or stake to support your snare.

Time. Five minutes at any skill level.

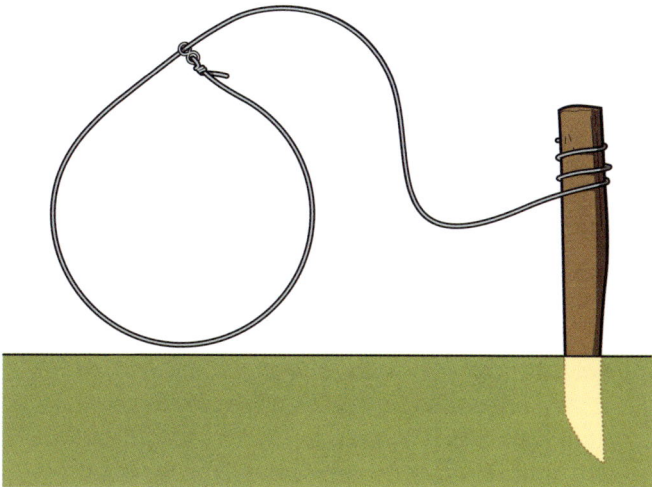

Instructions

1. Form a tiny loop at one end of the wire by making a bend in the wire and wrapping it around itself. The loop should be just large enough for the wire to pass through it freely.

2. After making the small loop, prepare the wire to form a smooth curve by grabbing both ends of the wire and passing it around a small tree branch. Gently move the wire back and forth like you are trying to saw the tree branch with it. This process can be skipped if you are using cable wire.

3. Once you have prepared the wire, take the other end of the wire and pass it through the small loop that you previously created, thus forming your snare loop.

4. Gently tighten the loop down until it is only slightly larger than the animal's head. If done correctly, the wire wants to spring closed rather than open. This step is called "loading the snare."

5. Select your location to set the snare and fasten the free end to a sturdy branch or a stake. This snare trap technique can be incorporated into spring poles as well. Place your snares along small game trails, near animal burrows, or near waterways. The animal must pass through the snare loop, so you will need to find or build a choke point to drive the animal through the loop.

Cleaning/cooking. If set properly, the wire snare trap does little damage to your target's organs and typically dispatches the animal. No special precautions are needed when cleaning your animal. Making a stew in a survival situation is always best so that you can consume the broth and not waste any nutrients or calories. Snap bones and boil them with the rest of the cleaned animal carcass to enjoy the benefits of bone broth.

Twitch-Up Bird Snare Trap

Uses. This trap is notable for its versatility and can be used for birds and other small game. Bird traps are best set in areas where bird activity is high, such as open fields with small trees.

Materials. You will need a spring pole, cordage, a snare loop, and a variety of sticks including two "Y" shaped sticks and a 10-inch stick for the support structure, as well as a stout 18-inch stick, a toggle stick, a 10- to 12-inch trigger stick, and four small sticks to keep the snare loop off the ground. Bait your trap with nuts, grains, a small shiny object, or a convenient perch.

> *A spring pole is the engine in an active trap. It is a sturdy, bendable tree or branch attached to the snare wire. When the tension on the pole is released, or the trap is triggered, the pole springs up quickly to activate the snare.*

Time. Five to 10 minutes at any skill level.

Instructions

This trap uses a spring pole or counterweight, but when trapping birds, the spring pole does not require a large amount of tension and does not have to hoist the animal off the ground.

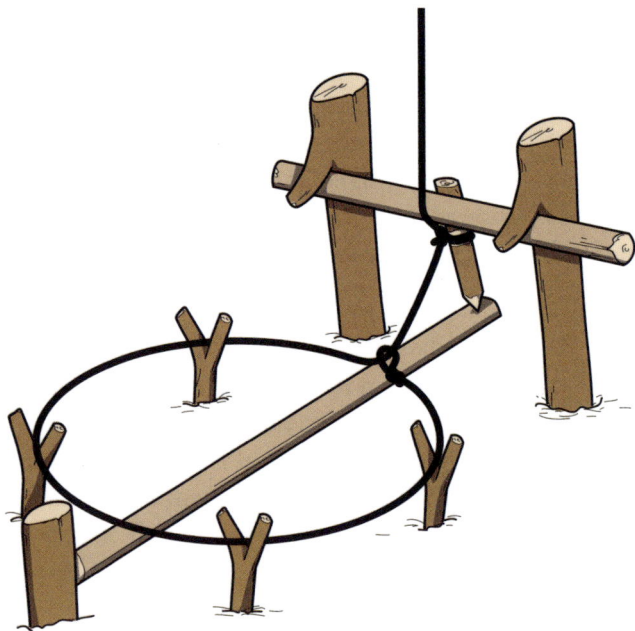

1. Once you have located an area with a suit-able spring pole, tie in your snare setup and toggle. (This snare setup is discussed in chapter 4 under "Tying a Noose to Create a Locking Trapper's Knot.")

2. Next, locate two sturdy "Y"-shaped sticks.

3. Drive the "Y" sticks into the ground, about 8 to 10 inches apart, the top of the "Y" facing toward the earth. Drive the sticks in deep enough that they will not pull out.

4. Using another stout stick, roughly 18 inches long, whittle one end into a point and drive it into the ground about 18 inches in front of and in between the "Y" sticks.

5. Then, wedge a stick between the two notches in the "Y" sticks, and while holding it in place, set the toggle so that it wants to move toward the stout stick that you placed in the previous step. The top end of the toggle should bind up against the stick that you placed in the "Y" notches and keep it from falling to the ground.

6. Place another stick, your trigger stick, so that it rests against the stout stick and the toggle. This trigger stick will prevent the toggle from moving and set the snare.

7. Poke four small sticks into the ground in a square around the trigger stick, which will hold your snare loop off the ground.

8. Once these sticks are placed, carefully rest the snare loop on top of them so that the loop also rests gently on the trigger stick.

9. Bait the ground under the loop with grains, fruit, shiny objects, meat, or nuts.

Cleaning/cooking. This trap does little to no damage to your target; no special precautions are needed when cleaning the animal to eat. As this trap is typically a foothold trap, the animal will probably still be alive when you check your trap. If you have caught a bird, grab it with your hands and calm it before snapping its neck. Otherwise, use a long stick as a spear or club.

Simple Twitch-Up Snare Trap

Uses. This simple 90-degree twitch-up snare is another versatile and easy-to-build trap. Commonly used to catch small game, this trap can also be used for birds, larger game, and fish. The simple twitch-up snare requires the use of a spring pole or counterweight and a snare loop for land- and air-based animals; for fish, you can use fishing line and a hook in place of the snare loop.

Materials. One 12- to 18-inch wooden stake and one 3- to 6-inch wooden stake, snare wire, and spring pole.

Time. Five to 10 minutes at any skill level.

Instructions

1. After carving a 90-degree notch into a long wooden stake, drive the stake into the ground.

2. Fasten a second, shorter wooden stake with a similar 90-degree notch to the spring pole. Attach the snare wire or fishing line to the spring pole line just above the second wooden stake.

3. Holding the second wooden stake, bend the spring pole down and latch the two notches together.

4. Carefully place your snare or fishing line in the location desired, build a funnel (if necessary), and walk away. This trap is best placed along small game trails, near or in front of animal burrows or

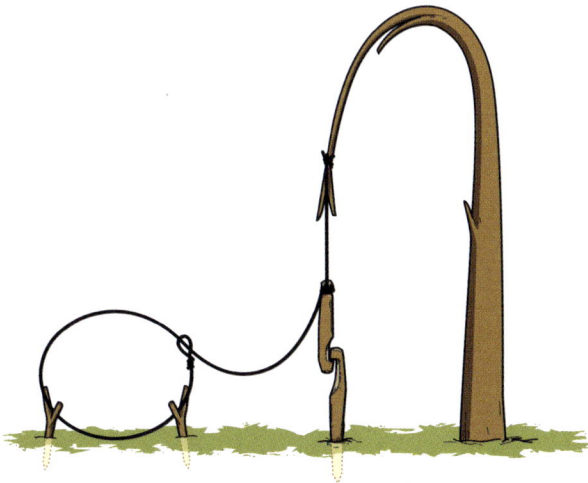

dens, or near waterways. The simple twitch-up snare relies on the animal to pass through the snare loop, so you will either set up the trap at a choke point or build a natural-looking funnel system that will drive the animal through the loop.

A variation of this trap requires no carving. Instead of carving 90-degree notches, look for two stout sticks that "Y" to form what looks like the number "7." The stake driven into the ground will be an upright "7," whereas the one attached to the spring pole will be an upside down "7" or an "L."

Cleaning/cooking. This trap does little to no damage to your target's organs and tends to dispatch the animal if set properly. No special precautions need to be taken when cleaning your animal.

Fish Basket Trap

Uses. The fish basket trap is best used in water, but in one lucky situation, I used it to catch a rabbit. No matter your level of expertise, this trap will take several hours to build. Though it takes a considerable amount of time, the rewards of this trap are great, as fish are one of the best natural sources of nutrients, fats, and calories.

Materials. Many long branches or vines. Plant materials from grape vines or willow stalks are most commonly used.

Time. One to two days for an experienced trapper.

Instructions

A fish basket trap is comprised of two main components: the first being a large basket and the second being a funnel that sits in the mouth of the basket.

1. To create the basket, lash together an uneven number of spokes and weave vines or stalks through the spokes, bending the spokes up as you go to form a basket shape.

2. Build the funnel using a similar method, but leave an opening at both ends for the fish to pass through. The smaller opening of the funnel should be just large enough to fit your hand

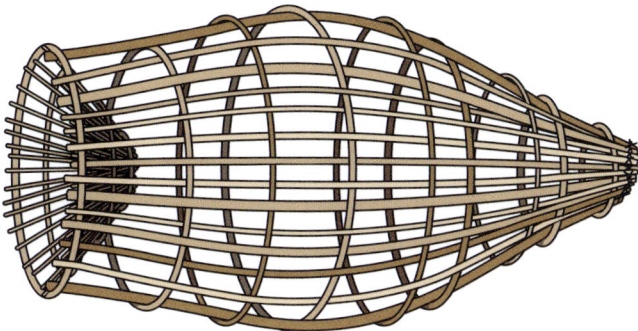

through and smaller still if the fish you are catching are smaller than your hand.

3. Sharpen the spokes at this end to deter fish from swimming out once they enter the basket.

4. When both components are completed, place the funnel on or into the basket and lash the funnel in place with small vines or willow reeds.

5. Place your trap in ponds, lakes, slow-moving currents, or oceans so that the opening of the funnel is to the side and the trap is completely submerged in the water.

6. Place rocks inside the trap to anchor it to the ground, or drive stakes through the trap to secure it to the bottom of the stream or pond.

7. Set your trap, then walk away to perform other duties. Check the trap at the end of each day. If food is not a priority, you can leave this trap untouched for longer.

Cleaning/cooking. You don't need to be concerned about cleaning or cooking your catch, as a basket trap typically catches the fish alive. Remove the entrails of the fish and save them as bait. Look for roe (fish eggs) as you clean the fish. Roe is edible and highly nutritious. Fish heads contain a lot of meat, so don't discard them. Instead, put the heads in the pot with the rest of your stew. Be cautious about small, sharp bones as you eat.

Paiute Deadfall

Uses. The Paiute deadfall is an active trap typically used to catch small game and rodents. This trap can be scaled up or down to match the size of your game and can be used in any environment. Typical targets are animals from 2 to 20 pounds, like squirrels, raccoons, or marmots.

Materials. Cordage (man-made or natural), a large flat rock or log, two sturdy support sticks about 10 inches long, a trigger stick, and one toggle. Plan to bait your trap with appropriate bait for your target.

Time. The first time you build this trap, you will need an hour. But with practice, you will be able to build this trap in 5 to 10 minutes.

Instructions

1. The deadfall for this trap can be a large flat rock, a log, or a group of logs lashed together. A rock is the best option. If you are using logs, they should weigh at least three times the weight of the animal that you intend to trap. If you cannot find a heavy enough log, lash smaller logs together to create a platform and stack rocks on top of them until you reach a sufficient weight. Locating the appropriate deadfall is often the most difficult part of building this trap. When setting the trap, be careful not to place your hand or other body parts under the deadfall.

2. Whittle the support sticks on one end to form a wedge shape. The other end should have a clean perpendicular cut across the stick.

3. To set this trap, tie a short length of cordage (about 10 inches) to the flat end of one of the support sticks.

4. Tie the other end of the cordage to the middle of your toggle.

5. On the end of the support stick, opposite of where you tied the cordage, move about two-thirds of the way down the stick and carve an elongated notch that the whittled end of the other support stick will fit into.

6. Place your other support stick upright at the edge of your deadfall as it lies flat on the ground. When set up, this support stick should lean slightly toward the deadfall.

7. Place the notch that you carved over the upright stick, flip the toggle and cordage around the upright stick, and hold it in place with your thumb.

8. Lift the deadfall and balance it on the very edge of the whittled end of the support stick that has the cordage tied to the other end. This step will take practice.

9. Once you have the balance correct, wedge a baited trigger stick between the lower back of the rock and the toggle.

Cleaning/cooking. The Paiute deadfall is a crushing trap, which means the trap can potentially damage the animal's internal organs. When cleaning the animal, check to see if the stomach or bladder have been ruptured. If you are not consuming the meat immediately after the trap was triggered, do not eat the meat around the abdomen area. Either way, the carcass should be rinsed thoroughly and cooked completely.

Fishing

This section outlines the basics of fishing—catching, preparing, and cooking—for survival. Fishing can be relaxing when done for leisure, but when you are trying to survive, you should not spend much time waiting for fish to bite. Set fish traps and then tend to other duties like building fire and shelter.

Angling

Fish prefer slow-moving waters where they can feed on insects. A good fishing hole is a deep area in a stream, where the current slows and forms swirls in the water, called eddies. Aim to land your bait in an eddy. If you are fishing in a lake or other large body of water, look for shaded areas and focus your fishing hours to early in the morning. Wear ultraviolet-protectant polarized sunglasses to reduce glare off the water and to spot fish with ease. When you are fishing, avoid fast movements or loud sounds, and try to avoid casting your shadow over the water. These actions will spook fish.

All this being said, in a survival scenario, your time is better spent making fish traps than angling. If you must spend time angling, designate an hour or two in the early morning as the sun comes up over the horizon. While you are angling, study the water and the environment around you, which will help you when you are setting up your fishing traps. The only time angling is not a waste of time is if you are consistently catching fish. If you are catching fish, catch as many as you possibly can, but you will need to smoke or preserve anything that you don't eat right away.

Hand Fishing

Hand fishing can be very successful in shallow, slow-moving streams. A friend and I once caught 30 fish and more than 50 crawdads by hand in a small mountain stream. The task took an entire day and involved getting very wet, but the rewards were far better than any I have ever had angling.

When the sun is at its fullest and the water is warm, fish will retreat to hiding spots under rocks or overhangs in the water. During this time, fish very rarely come out to feed. However, if you go to them, they are easy to catch.

To catch fish by hand, move slowly upstream while walking or crawling in the water. You will become soaking wet, so do not attempt this if the weather is too cold. Slowly slide your hand under every rock, and into every crevice where fish may be hiding. If you move slowly enough, the fish will not get spooked and will let you touch them. Slide your hand underneath the fish to its belly, slowly work your hand forward until you locate its gills, then hook your finger through the gills and slowly pull the fish out of the water. You may also be able to pin a fish with one hand as you grab its gills with the other.

Do not attempt hand fishing in deep or fast-moving streams. If you are in an area with snake-infested waters, hand fishing is dangerous. Be wary of large rocks that can shift and trap your hand beneath them.

Bait

If you have a fishing tackle box or a decent survival fishing kit, you will have artificial bait. But artificial bait is not always the best bait available. Check your supplies for food you can use; search the bottom of your pack for remnants of old snacks like raisins, bits of candy, dog food, or cigarette butts. If you need to catch a fish to survive, give everything a try. In addition to what you have in your kit or pack, flip over rocks to find beetles, crickets, grubs, worms, and spiders. When gathering insects, try not to kill them. Fish prefer fresh insects that are still moving on the hook.

Experiment with different types of bait, and once you catch a fish, open up its stomach to see what it has been eating for clues on what bait will be successful.

Improvised Hooks and Line

The internal strands of paracord can be used as improvised fishing line. If you do not have anything, fashion a line out of plant materials or use traps like a fishing basket.

Creating a hook is far easier than creating line. You can use common materials like safety pins, paperclips, or pull tabs from cans. If natural materials are your only option, look for small joints of branches with a hooked shape. Sharpen one end of a tiny branch and make a notch hole on the other to attach your line to. You can also fashion hooks out of thorns or small bones.

A gorge hook can also be used, which is a tiny, straight stick or other material that has been sharpened on both ends. Place the bait on the gorge hook in a manner that causes the hook to lie flat and in line with the fishing line. When the fish swallows the bait and you pull at the right moment, the gorge will turn sideways and lodge in the throat of the fish. If you can keep constant tension on the line, you may be able to pull the fish in.

Just as you should for any survival skill, practice making fishing hooks in a controlled environment.

Gill Nets and Fishing Spears

A gill net is a vertical panel of netting that hangs from the surface of the water down in a straight line. You can make a gill net out of bank line or the inner strands of paracord. Once you have created the net, stretch it across the stream to cover as much of the stream as possible. Drive stakes into the riverbank, as well as out into the water, to hold the net open. When stretching your net across the stream, don't stretch it too tightly. Leaving the net a little bit loose allows for a better chance for the fish to become tangled.

You can simply let the net sit, or you can move upstream and beat the water with a stick to drive fish toward the net.

Consider creating a spear to try and spear fish as you drive the fish toward your net. A fish spear should be at least your height or up to twice your height for maximum reach. The spear end should have multiple very small, very sharp points. Use the spear to thrust at fish or prod underneath rocks as you move downstream. When using a fishing spear, never walk with the point toward you or beneath your head height.

Fish Weir

A fish weir is a large fish trap that is built directly into the water. Fish can swim into the trap, but they are unable or unlikely to swim out. To build a fish weir, use sticks, large rocks, and other debris to form a "V"-shaped wall that channels the fish into an area that is difficult for them to escape. When building your weir, do not completely block, or dam, the flow of water. You just need to block any holes that are large enough for the fish to escape. Use bait or the guts of fish you have previously caught to lure fish into your weir. To speed up the process, move upstream and drive fish down toward your weir. When checking your trap, block the entryway into the cage or use a fishing spear or other instrument to dispatch the fish that are trapped.

Ice Fishing

When ice fishing, the best practice is to chip an 8- to 12-inch-diameter hole in the ice using your knife or another tool, then drop a weighted line down into the hole to determine the depth of the water. Once you know the depth of the water, position your baited hook about halfway down. The best bait for ice fishing is often larva or minnows, but not all fish have read this book, so try lures and jigs if you have them. As discussed before, experiment with any bait you can find. If you are able, build a hut or shelter over your fishing hole for protection from the elements. Although early-morning fishing is best in other fishing practices, you should wait until mid-morning to begin fishing during the cold season and continue until late afternoon.

Be sure the ice is thick enough to safely hold your weight. Ice should be no less than four inches thick to safely support you. To avoid having to stand over the fishing hole, secure the end of your line to a large "Y" stick at the top of the hole. This stick needs to be large enough so that it cannot be dragged down into the hole. Prop the stick so that the portion of the "Y" that you attached the line to is sticking up in the air. When you come back to check your fishing hole, if the stick is no longer in the air, you had a strike. Clear the hole of ice and pull in your line.

Preparing Fish

Preparing or cleaning a fish can be a messy task but is well worth it. Waste nothing on the fish. Use what you don't eat as chum or bait to catch your next fish, or use it in a land trap.

Begin by descaling your fish. You don't need to descale fish with small scales, like trout, but other fish have large, bony scales that you need to remove. Scrape the back side of your knife forward from tail to head until the scales are removed from the entire body. Save the scales for your chum.

Now, locate the anus of the fish and insert the tip of your knife, blade facing out. Carefully cut up toward the head to open the belly. Unlike with other animals, you do not need to be overly concerned with rupturing the stomach. Continue cutting all the way up to the gills using just the tip of your knife.

Reach into the belly with your hands, firmly grasp the organs, and tear them out. Put the guts in your chum pile. Look for roe as you remove the organs. Roe is full of great nutrients and quite tasty; remove the roe and keep it with the edible portion of the fish.

Keep the head on the fish while you cook it to avoid losing valuable nutrients. If you choose, you can remove the lower jaw and bones in the gills to save you from having to pick them out of your stew later.

Cooking Fish

In a survival situation, you can cook fish a couple of ways, each with its own merits.

Cooking pot. Cooking with this tool will ensure the most calories and nutrients. To do so, put the entire cleaned fish in a cooking pot, including the head, eyes, and, if you are lucky, the roe. Fill your pot with water, and if you can find them, add some wild edibles to your pot. Place the pot over a hot fire and boil it until the meat falls off the bones. Gently stir your stew as you are cooking to help the meat part from the bones. Remove clean bones from the pot as you see them. Do not stir too fast or too hard, which will break the bones and make them more difficult to remove.

Skewer. This method works well and makes a tasty treat. However, calories are lost using this method. When the meat is cooked over a fire, the fats cook out and drip off.

To create a skewer, take the following steps:

1.   Gather three sticks: one thick stick (three to four feet long) and two short, thinner sticks (each about eight inches long).

2.   Carefully split the end of the long stick down the center with your knife. The length of the split should be only a few inches longer than the length of your fish.

3. Strip the bark from around the split in two large pieces, and set the bark aside.

4. Thread the long stick through the mouth of your fish until the stick goes past the tail. Firmly press the fish over the stick so that the belly of the fish wraps around both sides of the stick.

5. Take the two shorter sticks and pierce them through the flesh of the fish so that the shorter sticks penetrate both sides of the fish and also pass through the split you made in the long stick.

6. Using the bark that you previously removed, tie the split stick back together. This step will anchor the fish in place and keep it from spinning on your stick as you rotate it over the flames.

If you find any wild onions or other wild edibles, you can pack them inside your skewered fish to add flavor. If while eating your fish you find that some of it is not cooked all the way, continue eating the cooked portions while placing the uncooked portions back over the fire.

Edible Plants, Fruit, Fungi, and Flowers

Many plants are edible, and many are also poisonous. This section offers guidance on how you can learn to identify edible plants. Never place a plant in your mouth unless you know exactly what it is.

Don't Test It Out!

How do you figure out whether a plant, fruit, or mushroom is edible? Military and some civilian instructors teach the concept of the "universal edibility test," which goes something like this:

Rub a bit of the plant on your skin, testing for contact poison. If the plant causes a reaction, don't eat it. If it passes the test, put a small portion of the plant on your lips and in your mouth, but spit it out and don't swallow. If you get a reaction, don't eat it. If the plant passes that test, swallow a small portion and wait several hours to see if you have a reaction. If you do, don't eat any more.

This test is absolutely not advisable. Two clear examples of the test's flaws are stinging nettle and golden banner. Stinging nettle instantly fails this test, but it is one of the most nutritious plants found in the wild if it is dried or boiled before consumption. Golden banner, on the other hand, passes every one of these tests, but as soon as you eat enough, you become violently ill and could die.

If you cannot identify the plant, do not put it in your mouth.

No edibility tests exist that I recommend. Do not rely on Internet forums or phone apps that claim to identify plants. Instead, purchase books from reputable authors and do the research yourself. Your life depends on it!

Learning to Identify Plants

To become a plant aficionado, obtain five books that cover the exact region that you wish to learn about. Do not rely on books that use hand drawings to identify plants. The best options are books with full-color photos of each plant for each season of the year.

Take your books, a notepad, and a pen on a walk until you find a plant that you wish to learn about. Sit down next to that plant and locate it in each of your books. Pay close attention to every tiny detail on the plant, including leaf shape and structure, leaf veins, number of petals on the flowers, number of stamens, and pattern of leaves. These details will help you note the subtle differences that distinguish plants from their lookalikes.

After you have found and read about your plant in every book, draw the plant. Draw it in the most detail that you can. Take notes. Take pictures that include your notes, the plant, and the plant's page from the book all in the same shot.

Enroll in a class with a wild plant expert and share your pictures with them. Ask them to identify and confirm your identification of the plant.

Take your friends out to look at the plant. Every time you see that plant, stop and talk about it. Once you have gotten to the point at which the world around you is annoyed with that plant, you will never forget what that plant is. You are now safe to put that plant into your mouth, assuming it is not a poisonous plant!

Fruit

Exercise great caution when foraging for fruit in the wild. Not all fruits are edible. The general rule is that 80 percent of blue and black berries are edible, 50 percent of red berries are edible, and 20 percent of white berries are edible.

When picking a fruit, be aware of other animals in the area. Inspect each piece of fruit to be sure that no animal or bird droppings are on the fruit. If so, wash the fruit thoroughly or cook it.

Just like with leafy plants, be wary of eating any fruit that you cannot confidently identify. If you are unsure of the type of berry, do not mix it with berries that you have previously identified as safe.

Pay special attention to children, who like placing brightly colored objects like berries into their mouths.

Common edible fruits and berries include elderberry (but not Rocky Mountain elderberry), cloudberry, huckleberry, gooseberry, salmonberries, blackberry, bearberry, chokecherry, apples, rose hips, raspberries, blueberries, currants, and prickly pear cactus. A great start is to learn about all of these common fruits and how to identify them and the plants on which they grow.

POISONOUS PLANT ENCOUNTERS

If you think you have ingested something poisonous and medical help is not available, induce vomiting. Make a charcoal slurry by powdering the black charcoal from your extinguished fire and combining it with just enough water to make it drinkable. Make sure no hot coals are in your cup, then drink the slurry quickly. Your body will expel the charcoal, which will have absorbed some of the toxins.

If you have a wild plant book, look up the plant you have ingested for advice on natural remedies. For example, coffee has been used as an antidote to the poisonous hemlock and water hemlock, although it is not a foolproof remedy to these dangerous plants. Always exercise caution when using natural remedies, and seek professional medical support immediately.

If you come into contact with poison ivy, do not scratch the rash, as you will spread the oils around. If you are able to locate jewelweed, its sap can counteract the oils of the poison ivy. Another natural remedy for poison ivy is sticky gumweed, which will not stop the itch, but its sticky sap will prevent the oils from spreading and remind you not to scratch. For poison ivy and other skin irritants, take an antihistamine to relieve symptoms. You can also apply oatmeal mixed with cool water to help soothe the itch and absorb some of the oils.

Toxic red baneberries.

Edible gooseberries.

Edible elderberries.

Toxic Rocky Mountain elderberries.

Fungi

Although mushrooms don't have a lot of calories, they are full of vitamins and minerals and can be super tasty if you find ones that are safe to consume.

Most mushrooms have a cap and a stalk or stem. When identifying these mushrooms, first check whether the underside of the cap has gills or a denser surface with pores. Once you have observed the underside of the cap, note the texture of the stalk, the shape of the gills (if present), the consistency of the cap, and the color of the mushroom's spores. These key identifying features will help you determine whether a mushroom is edible. Obtain a good book and study it well.

Note the color and texture of a mushroom's cap and stalk to begin identifying it.

Gills on the underside of a mushroom cap.

Pores on the underside of a mushroom cap.

Of course, before you can identify mushrooms, you must find them. Mushrooms pop up in the spring and fall when temperatures are mild. The ground needs to be warm yet moist for mushrooms to flourish. They are typically found in forests, away from direct sunlight, though some varieties can also be found in open fields.

Flowers

Flowers can be edible, have medicinal uses, be high in vitamin C and other vitamins and minerals, and be used to make inks and dyes.

When observing flowers to determine whether they are edible, watch for details like color, number of petals and stamens, solitary flowers or clusters of flowers, and the presence of sepals or bracts. Flowers have many identifying features, and they can be the easiest way to identify a plant. However, the flowers are only on a plant for a short time, so you should know how to identify plants before the flower blooms and after it falls to the ground.

Although the color is usually the first thing that you notice about a flower, it is also the least important, as the color of a flower can vary in the same species of plant. Every detail of that flower is important and can be used to determine the species. For instance, several different mustard plants belong to the *Cruciferae* family. *Cruciferae* is associated with the word "cross"; all mustard flowers have four petals.

Golden banner flowers. Golden banner
is poisonous and should not be consumed.

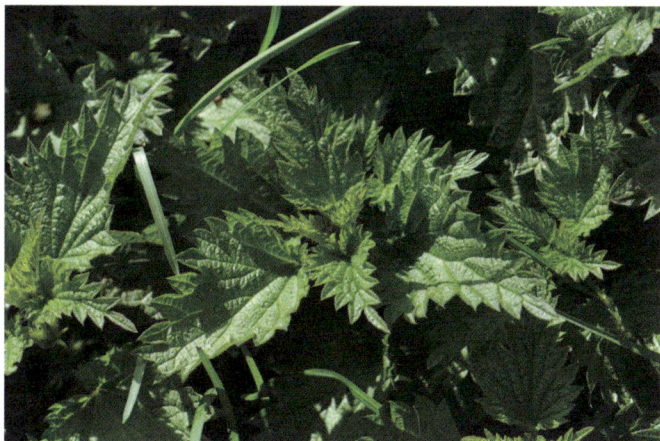

Stinging nettle. Prepare stinging nettle
for safe consumption by drying or boiling it.

Harvest flowers ethically. If you pick a flower, and it's the only one or one of few in an area, you are harming its ability to reproduce. Furthermore, you are removing a food source for bees and other insects.

Staying Safe

Wild animals, though amazing to see, can be dangerous. You should know which animals are common in the areas where you adventure and understand their behaviors and threat displays. Never leave out food, toothpaste, deodorant, or anything with a pungent odor. Do not take these items into your tent or shelter. Wash your hands and face after eating and before you crawl into bed.

Bear Encounters

Bear encounters are common in the wild. Your response to a bear should be specific to the type of bear you meet. That said, the same rules apply to any species of bear. If you see a cub, the momma bear is very close by, watching you. Never approach a cub or let a cub approach you. Do not try to scare the cub away. Instead, back away slowly and get out of the area. If you have any, drop food to distract the cub.

Brown Bears/Grizzly Bears. You can identify a brown bear by the large hump on its back. If you encounter such a bear, do not run. You will not outrun a bear. Walk away slowly if the bear is not approaching you, but do not turn your back. If the bear charges, stand your ground. Brown bears are territorial and are most likely defending their turf rather than considering you to be prey. Avoid direct eye contact, as brown bears consider it a sign of aggression. A yawning brown bear or one that is pawing at the ground is agitated. Back away slowly. Don't scream or yell. Speak in a soft, monotone voice and wave your arms to let the animal know you are human. Huddle in a group if you are with others. If you have pepper spray, prepare to use it if the bear charges to within 25 feet of where you're standing.

If the animal makes contact, curl into a ball on your side, or lie flat on your stomach. Play dead, but protect your head with your arms and hands. Try not to panic; remain as quiet as possible until the attack ends. Be sure the bear has left the area before getting up to seek help.

Black Bears. Black bears can be brown, cinnamon, or blond in color. They lack a hump on their back. If you are adventuring in black bear country, carry bear pepper spray. As with the grizzly bear, pepper spray should be your first line of defense in a bear attack. If you encounter a black bear, stand your ground and make lots of noise. Never turn and run. Black bears often bluff when attacking. If you show them you mean business, they may lose interest. Huddle in a group if you are with others. Do not climb a tree in an attempt to escape from a bear, as black bears are excellent climbers.

If a black bear attacks, fight back; it intends to eat you. Use anything and everything as a weapon—rocks, sticks, fists, and your teeth. Aim your blows on the bear's face, particularly the eyes and snout. When a black bear sees that its prey is willing to fight to the death, it'll usually give up.

Mountain Lion Encounters

Mountain lions and other large cats are very stealthy. Pay attention to the environment around you. If the forest around you was once full of chirping birds and chattering squirrels but has gone eerily quiet, a large cat or other predator is likely in the area.

Stay alert while in mountain lion country. The best offense is a good defense. Be extra alert when you crouch, sit, or kneel, as mountain lions consider this position a good opportunity to pounce. On the other hand, mountain lions do not see standing humans as prey. Stand tall. Do not investigate dead animals in the brush, and leave the area quickly if you discover one. Keep a close eye on children, pets, and the smallest members in your party when venturing in mountain lion country.

If you encounter a mountain lion, remain calm and back away slowly. Do not run. You cannot outrun a large cat, and running may stimulate the animal's instinct to chase you. Maintain eye contact with the cat and do not turn your back.

If the mountain lion approaches you, make yourself appear larger by raising your arms and opening your jacket. Wave your arms and speak in a loud, firm voice. Huddle in groups if you are with others. Throw branches, stones, or whatever you can find. Don't be easy prey; fight back.

Coyote and Wild Dog Encounters

Coyotes usually live in families, but when hunting, they tend to travel solo. However, coyotes have been known to send in a decoy to draw out your pet to come play or pursue them. Once your pet chases that coyote away from you, the rest of the pack pounces. Do not let your children or pets stray away from you if a coyote is present. The same is true of feral dogs, which are a bigger threat to humans than coyotes and should be treated accordingly.

Coyotes scavenge or hunt small game, but if they are hungry enough, they will risk trying for larger game like humans. Do not show fear to coyotes or wild dogs. They usually will not attack if they think you are a serious threat. Stay calm, make yourself big, yell, pick up a large stick, and be aggressive. Never run, but you may need to leave their territory, especially if you have stumbled upon a den. Back away slowly and leave the area as soon as possible. Wild dogs are far more aggressive and tend to travel in packs. Step up your own aggression and fight back.

Snake Encounters

Your best option when dealing with snake encounters is to avoid them. Still, you should know how to identify venomous snakes in your area. Most land-based snakes, like rattlesnakes and copperheads, are non-aggressive and want to be left alone. Rattlesnakes will usually give you a warning that they are there. Semiaquatic snakes like cottonmouths (also called water moccasins) are more aggressive and may pursue you if they feel threatened.

Key identifying differences between venomous and non-venomous snakes include:

VENOMOUS	NON-VENOMOUS
Elliptical pupil	Rounded pupil
Triangular head	Rounded head
Two large fangs	Small teeth (no large fangs)
Pit vipers have a pit beneath the nostril	No pit beneath the nostril

Venomous coral snakes, cobras, mambas, and tiger snakes are an exception to these rules as they have rounded pupils and heads. The coloring of these snakes may be their easiest identifying feature, but lookalikes always exist. If you are in an area known to have these snakes and you are not familiar with them, assume every snake you encounter is venomous. That doesn't mean kill it. Just leave it alone.

To avoid encountering snakes, avoid tall grasses. Before stepping over logs or rocks, check the opposite side. When traveling in groups, the second person in line is usually the one to get bit. Snakes can climb trees. Keep your wits about you when traveling through a thick forest. Avoid sticking your hands in holes or crevices. Leave dead snakes alone! Even a dead snake's head can bite you and inject venom. Sleep off the ground or in a tent whenever possible. Avoid sleeping in tall grasses, rocky areas, or near large logs. Wear heavy boots and pants that cannot be penetrated by fangs.

If bitten by a snake, remain calm. Remove any jewelry in case of swelling. Do not try to suck out the venom, bleed the wound, or administer ice packs or tourniquets. Your best bet is to evacuate and seek immediate medical attention.

Encounters with Deer, Elk, Moose, and Other Herbivores

Cartoons portray animals like moose and deer as friendly, which is perhaps why so many people, especially children, are injured by them each year. Don't feed these animals or approach them; doing so is highly dangerous for both you and the animal and is also illegal. Deer and elk in the wild can be aggressive, and moose are temperamental and very aggressive.

If you encounter a moose, keep your distance, and, if possible, place a barrier like a large tree or boulder between you and the animal. If the moose turns and squares up to you, make loud noises to scare it away. If it does not scare, then you should back away quickly.

Insect Encounters

You cannot get away from insects, but you can make attempts at keeping them away from you. Whenever possible, use insect repellent, and if you are severely allergic, be sure to carry your epinephrine injections with you. Stock an antihistamine like Benadryl in your medical kit to slow swelling or rashes that may occur from insect bites or stings. Permethrin is a very effective insecticide, but it should not be applied directly to your skin. Treat clothing with permethrin before you get dressed.

Insects dislike smoke. If flying insects are driving you crazy, build a smoky fire to keep them away. You can also set fire to a bundle of sage or find a rotted piece of wood, both of which will smolder for a long time and generate a lot of smoke. Set the burning sage or wood near you or carry it with you as a mobile bug repellent, but be mindful of hot sparks or ash that could burn you or start a wildfire.

Bees. If you are stung by a bee and the stinger still remains in your skin, grabbing and pulling the stinger will release more venom into your body. Instead, use your knife or a credit card to scrape off the stinger from the side.

Wasps. Wasps can be aggressive, so do your best to avoid them. If you see a wasps' nest, turn around and walk away. Our instinct is to swing at a wasp to get it to leave us alone. Although not a good idea, everyone tends to do it. If you happen to swing at a wasp while you are near its nest, the insect is going to come back with friends. Instead, remain still, move away without swinging at it, and protect your head and face.

Ticks. If a tick has buried its head under your skin, do not grab it and pull it off. Use tweezers to grasp the tick close to your skin and steadily but firmly pull up and away. Using a match or lighter to remove a tick is risky because doing so can cause the tick to expel its bodily fluid beneath your skin and cause an infection. Once you remove the tick, clean the area thoroughly.

Spiders and scorpions. To avoid spider bites and scorpion stings, never reach your hands under rocks if you need to flip them or pick them up. Instead, grasp the rock by the top first and roll it over to see what is hiding underneath.

CHAPTER SIX

NAVIGATION

Three general approaches to navigation are no-tech, low-tech, and high-tech. No-tech navigation uses the sun, stars, and celestial occurrences for orientation. Low-tech navigation is achieved through the use of a map and compass. Low-tech is the most reliable and safest method if you know how to use the tools. High-tech, of course, means the use of a GPS device or cell phone. These tools are very accurate under normal situations, but when the batteries die or you are without service, these tools will fail you. Due to modern technology, low-tech navigation is a much-overlooked skill but one that I find to be highly important when traveling into the backcountry. With the proper tools, a person can pinpoint their exact location on a map, anywhere in the world, and from there navigate with confidence.

Navigation is not a skill that you can pick up on the fly. Learn it before you need it, and stay in practice. This section will help you apply basic navigation techniques for wilderness adventures.

Finding North

Although you should always have a map and compass in your kit, you can navigate without them. The first step is determining which direction is north. No matter where you are in the world, the sun rises in the east and sets in the west. If you stand with the sunrise to your right, you are facing in a northerly direction. Behind you is south and to your left is west. Once you know which way is north, you can obtain a general bearing, or azimuth, toward where you want to travel.

> *Don't trust the popular saying "Moss grows on the north face of trees." Although this is sometimes true, moss can also grow on any side of a tree. And, if you're in the Southern Hemisphere, moss is more likely to be found on the south face of trees.*

If you are hopelessly lost and don't know where you need to travel, knowing which way is north won't help you very much. In most situations, the wisest course of action is to stay put until someone finds you. However, you may need to move from your location for some reason, as when you are running out of supplies or if your immediate location has become unsafe.

WHAT TO DO WHEN YOU'RE LOST: S.T.O.P.A.

S = Stay put. If you are in immediate danger, make an expedient plan to get out of harm's way. Once safe to do so, stop, sit down, and calm yourself. Don't make the situation worse by continuing on.

T = Think. Gather your wits and think about your situation. Assess your needs. Can you take care of your basic survival needs of food, fire, shelter, water, and health? Are you or anyone in your party hurt? Is anybody missing? If so, call out but don't run off looking. Stay put. Administer first aid as needed.

O = Observe. Observe your surroundings for immediate dangers. What gear do you have with you and what resources are around you?

P = Plan. Make a plan and stick to it. What needs to be done to increase your success of survival or to increase your chances of being found? Include contingency plans.

A = Act. S.T.O.P. before you act! Then put your plan into motion. If your situation changes, S.T.O.P. again!

Measuring Distance Traveled on Foot

Pace count. In the wilderness, you can track how much distance you have traveled by keeping track of your paces. Your pace count is the number of paces it takes you to travel 100 meters (328 feet). Determine your pace count by marking out 100 meters on level ground. If you are unable to mark out 100 meters using a tape measure, use a constant that you do know—such as your height—to determine an approximate distance. Cut a piece of string or a stick to your height and use it to measure out approximately 100 meters.

At your starting point, take two steps in a normal fashion. Walk like you would if you were casually walking down a sidewalk. When your second foot hits the ground, that is one pace. Keep walking, counting every other footstep until you reach 100 meters. Best practice is to walk the same path three times and take the average pace count. Your pace will change if you are traveling uphill, downhill, over rugged terrain, or with a heavy load. You should figure out your pace count in a controlled environment before you set out on an adventure. Memorize your pace count and write it down to keep in your navigation kit.

Once you have determined your level ground pace count, measure out 100 meters on a gradual uphill slope as well as a steep uphill slope. Using the same method, record your pace count for walking both uphill and downhill. Record your count without a load on and also with your fully loaded backpack on.

Knowing your pace count will help you track the distance that you have traveled. Of course, you may find counting steps in your head over a long period of time difficult, which is why I recommend that you carry ranger beads in your navigation kit. If you prefer a higher-tech option, fitness trackers and smartphones can also be used to count your steps.

RANGER BEADS

Ranger beads are a short length of string with a knot tied in the middle. On one side of the center knot are four beads. On the other side of the knot are nine beads. The nine beads each represent 100 meters. The four beads each represent 1,000 meters.

When starting out, slide all of the beads to the bottom, outside the knots. Every time you take your calculated pace count steps, move one of the nine beads to the center knot. Once all nine beads have been moved upward, your next set of pace count steps will be 1,000 meters. You will then slide one of the four beads to the center knot and return the nine beads to the bottom. You have walked 1,000 meters. Repeat. When you slide the second of your four beads up, you have walked 2,000 meters.

Dead reckoning. When you must travel but don't know where you're going and lack a map and compass, dead reckoning is a useful tactic. Dead reckoning is effective in any environment. You simply choose a direction to travel, find the farthest distinguishable landmark in that direction, and walk toward it.

Before you begin traveling toward your landmark, estimate the distance to that spot. Keep track of your paces as you walk toward your destination to help you gauge distance traveled. Once underway, turn around often and take note of where you came from. Looking behind you allows you to see what your starting point looks like so that you can return, should you need to. Once you reach your destination, confirm it's where you want to be, then pick your next destination and repeat this process.

Using a Compass

You can choose from several types of compasses. I recommend a compass that has, at a minimum, a housing, a bezel ring, an index line, and a scale. Lensatic and orienteering compasses are your best options.

Determining the direction you want to go is also called "shooting an azimuth." To begin, hold the compass level, keeping it level throughout your navigation. Confirm no metal objects are near the compass, as they can interfere with your reading. Once the needle is able to spin freely, turn your body to face the same direction that the needle

Lensatic compass.

Orienteering compass.

is pointing. You are now facing Magnetic North and are oriented to your environment. If you have a map, you can orient your map to the environment as well. Orienting your map requires a couple extra steps due to "declination," which is discussed on the following page.

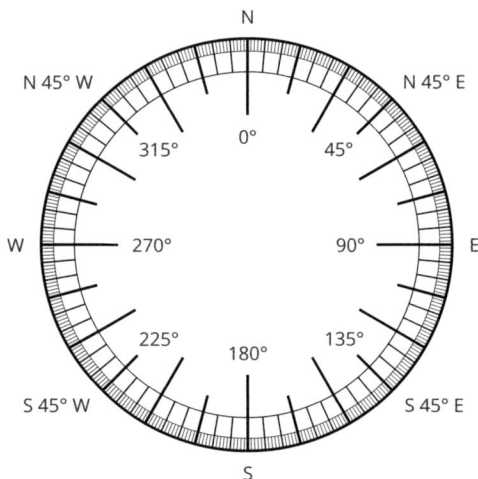

North might not be the direction you want to travel. Your azimuth is the angle on the compass for the direction that you want to go. For example, if you want to head northwest, your azimuth is 315 degrees.

To set the azimuth of your compass, turn the compass base toward the direction you wish to travel (in this case, 315 degrees) and line up the sights to point in the direction you want to go. Now, read the number that is beneath the fixed black index line. This is your azimuth. As you walk, stop occasionally to make sure you are continuing on the same azimuth. You can use a combination of shooting your azimuth and dead reckoning to stay on target.

Your compass does not point toward the North Pole; it points toward the northern magnetic field (Magnetic North) of Earth, which is a long ways from the North Pole (True North). Maps are oriented toward True North. To line up your map and compass, you will use declination.

Declination is the difference in angle from where the needle on your compass is pointing (Magnetic North) compared to the geographical North Pole (True North). If you lay your compass down on the map without taking declination into account, your map will not accurately line up with your compass.

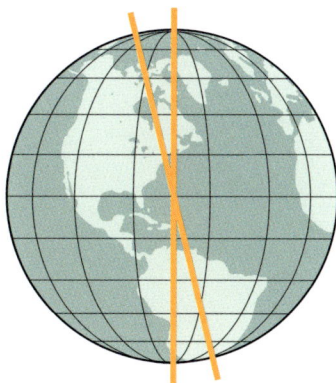

Your compass points to Magnetic North, which is a long way from the North Pole, or True North.

Declination changes depending on where you are in the world and also changes over time. A good map will tell you, in its legend, what you need to do to adjust for declination, though an old map might have outdated information. Before you head into the wilderness, check the National Oceanic and Atmospheric Administration (NOAA) website for the most accurate magnetic declination.

Once you know the declination, you will add or subtract that declination each time you take a bearing or azimuth. A west declination (left of True North) is a negative number, whereas an east declination (right of True North) is a positive number.

Finding Yourself on a Map

To best determine your location on a map, you will need a good view of your surroundings. Once you can see far enough, you will use your tools to triangulate your position.

Select two notable landmarks, like high mountain peaks, distant ridgelines, low valleys, or large notable rock formations. Whatever you chose, each landmark should have memorable, distinct features, and your two landmarks should be at least 60 degrees apart from each other.

If you do not have a compass, turn your map until the terrain features line up. Using those terrain features as a reference, you can make a guess as to your location.

With a compass, you will be able to pinpoint your location. To start, adjust for declination. Once you have done this step, point the direction-of-travel arrow at your first chosen landmark, allowing your magnetic needle to point to Magnetic North. Now rotate the housing of your compass so that the orienting arrow lines up with the needle. Where the direction-of-travel arrow intersects the dial is your bearing to that landmark. Make note of this bearing.

Repeat the process with your second selected landmark, and take note of the bearing. Use the two bearings to triangulate your location.

To apply these bearings to your map, lay the map flat on the ground and place your compass on top of the map, without moving the compass housing. Align the compass needle with north on the map. Your direction-of-travel arrow should be pointing in the direction of your landmark on the map.

Find your first landmark on the map, and lay your compass so that the corner of the baseplate touches your landmark. Draw a line that follows your bearing using the ruler on the edge of the baseplate. Repeat the process using your second landmark and bearing. The two lines will intersect at your location.

Interpreting Maps and Terrain Features

To learn to identify and interpret terrain features on a map, obtain a good topographical map of an area with which you are familiar. Choose a location that has a lot of hills, valleys, and maybe a cliff or two. If you cannot find a good map, you can have a map printed of exactly the area you want. Many places online provide this service. If you are having trouble finding your desired location on the map, try thinking about what that location looks like from a bird's-eye view.

Acquaint yourself with the following features of your map:

Legend. You should look for the legend first. A good map will have a legend that explains what every symbol and color means on your map. The legend will also tell you when the map was made and the declination.

Legend colors. Maps use different colors to indicate different terrain features, including:

- Black—human-made structures (buildings, bridges)

- Red—roads or other human-made features

- Green—vegetation

- White—lack of vegetation or sparse vegetation

- Brown—contour lines

- Blue—water (ponds, rivers, streams, ocean, sea)

Scale. Most maps sold in sporting goods stores use a scale of 1:63,360, which means that one inch on the map is equal to one mile on land. Although this measurement is easy to calculate, I prefer a 1:24,000 scale because it shows more detail. To obtain maps at this scale, I print my own maps from the Internet.

Grid coordinates. On the edge of the map, you will see small numbers next to the lines that run across the map. These are grid coordinates. Using this grid scale, every point on the map has an exact number. These numbers will either be in longitude and latitude, or in UTM (Universal Transverse Mercator) coordinates. UTM is a plane coordinate grid system using easting and northing numbers. Easting are the numbers on the horizontal axis (left/right) of the map, whereas northing numbers are on the vertical axis. UTM is widely used in land navigation, so you should learn this system. For example, the latitude/longitude coordinates of the Statue of Liberty are (40.689247°N, –74.044502°W). The UTM coordinates are (580,735.64 E, 4,504,700.38 N).

Contour lines. Contour lines are thick and thin wavy lines. Each line indicates a consistent elevation. If you look closely at the thickest of the lines, you will see the elevation where that line is located. The thick lines with elevation numbers are called "index lines." The thinner, unmarked lines are called "intermediate lines." Use the elevation markings to calculate the elevation of intermediate lines. The closer the lines, the steeper the terrain.

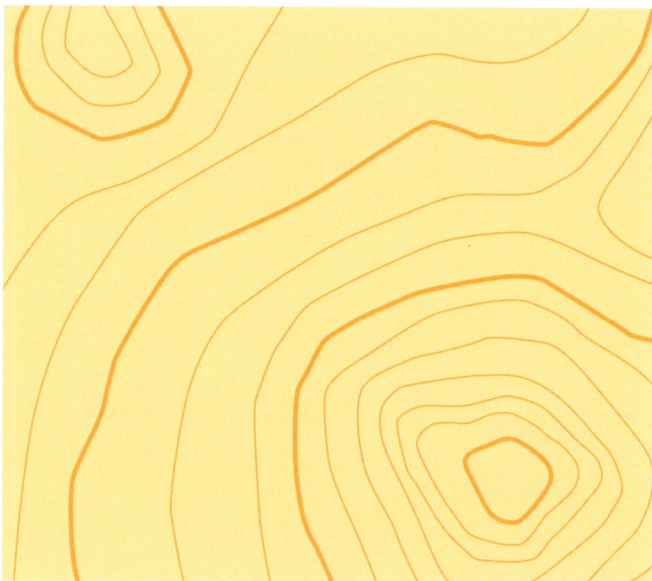

Use contour lines to gauge
the elevation and steepness of terrain.

Using the Night Sky to Navigate

The sun should be the first star you use for navigating, as you are safer traveling during the day. The exception to this rule is when you are navigating in arid climates (deserts); in that case, plan your route during the day prior to walking at night when the weather is cooler. Should you need to travel at night, however, you can use the moon and stars to navigate. Like the sun, the moon rises in the east and sets in the west. Use a crescent moon to determine south by drawing an imaginary line connecting the endpoints of the moon's crescent and continuing that line down to the Earth's horizon. The point where that line touches the horizon is south. If you are in the Southern Hemisphere, this point indicates north.

To use the stars to navigate, locate the Big Dipper, which will guide you to True North at any time of year. The Big Dipper gets its name because it resembles a ladle if you connect the stars with an imaginary line. If you extend the imaginary line from the two stars farthest from the handle's end, that line will point toward the North Star. The North Star is at True North. When looking for the North Star, you can double-check yourself by referring to the constellation Cassiopeia. Locate the middle point of the "W" shape of Cassiopeia, and draw an imaginary line straight across the horizon toward the Big Dipper. Where the imaginary line of the Big Dipper and the imaginary line from Cassiopeia intersect, you will find the North Star.

A common misconception is that the brightest light in the celestial sky is the North Star. In fact, the brightest points of light are most likely Venus or Mars. If you are unsure, look closely. Stars will twinkle, planets will not. And if you can discern color, Mars will be red and Venus blue.

Using the Sun to Measure Time

In a survival situation, knowing the exact time isn't important. However, you need to know how many hours of sunlight you have left in your day to give yourself enough time to set up camp before dark.

To gauge how many hours you have left in the day, start by finding a ridge or open area where you can clearly see the sun and the horizon that the sun will set behind. Face the sun and outstretch one arm fully, turning your hand so that your palm is toward you and your index finger is the top finger. Position the top of your index finger just beneath the sun.

Use your hand to block out the sun. Now, slowly move your hand down until the second or third knuckle of your index finger is just below the sun. Each finger of space between the sun and the horizon counts as 15 minutes.

For example, if you have one hour of daylight left, the top of your index finger should be just beneath the sun and the bottom of your little finger should sit on the horizon. If the space is less than four fingers, curl one finger at a time until the gap between the horizon and the sun is filled with your fingers. If the distance is greater than four fingers, use your other hand. If the distance is greater than two hands, put your top hand beneath your second hand and repeat the process until you reach the horizon.

WHEN YOU ARE LOST: FINDING YOURSELF OR HELPING OTHERS FIND YOU

Turn being "lost" into being "temporarily disoriented" by maintaining a calm mindset and following these steps to either find yourself or to help others find you.

Manage your time. It takes at least three hours to set up a crude camp that will cover your basic needs (though if you have a tarp, you can have a shelter in minutes). If you don't have a watch, use the sun to measure time.

If darkness is quickly approaching, your priority is gathering firewood to start a fire; you may have to sleep next to your campfire with no other amenities. If weather conditions are unfavorable, a waterproof shelter is a priority. Do not go to sleep cold.

Find yourself on the map. The techniques of terrain association and triangulation will help you reorient yourself. Look at the terrain features around you, imagine what they would look like on a map, then find matching features on the map itself. If you have a compass, you can orient yourself and your map to north. Without a compass, you can get a general direction by using the sun (see page 144).

To best determine your location on a map, you will need a good view of your surroundings. Once you can see far enough, you can use your tools to triangulate your position (see page 152).

Get noticed by rescuers. Don't signal to commercial airliners; they won't see you. Save your energy and resources for low-flying small planes, helicopters, or ground vehicles.

Standing in a clearing at higher elevation than the terrain around you will increase your chances of being seen and will allow you to see farther as well. Sounds from audible signaling devices like whistles carry farther from higher elevations. Bright colors and reflective surfaces are helpful.

Make a loud noise—give a blast from a whistle or a shot from a firearm. Do this three times, pause for 30 seconds, then repeat. Continue this process as often as possible until help arrives.

If your signal devices aren't getting the attention of your rescuers, build a large, maintainable signal fire. Three fires in a triangle is an international distress signal. If you suspect rescuers are close enough to see you, add green tree branches or any material that will produce a lot of smoke. The more smoke, the better, but be careful not to smother your fire.

CHAPTER SEVEN

APPLYING FIRST AID

When no one else is around, you are the first responder. Successfully applying first aid relies more on critical thinking skills and the ability to improvise than on having modern supplies. In the wild, you must be able to make use of any gear that you have on hand and may have to source what you need from the environment around you. Familiarize yourself with these first aid skills so that you can act quickly should you or a party member become injured.

This section discusses basic first aid techniques to treat the most common injuries that occur in the wild. These steps will help you stabilize your patient so that you can either wait for help to arrive or transport your patient to definitive care. This section does not substitute proper medical training, and I highly advise you to seek out wilderness first aid or wilderness first responder classes.

Before performing any treatment, pause to take a quick assessment of the patient and their surroundings. Your very first step is to make sure the area is safe for both you and the patient. Next, assess the patient using the M.A.R.C.H. protocol to prioritize treatment. This assessment should only take a minute to complete and will help you remember to check for the most life-threatening injuries in order of importance:

M = Massive hemorrhage. Is your patient losing a lot of blood? With massive bleeding, a person can bleed out faster than they can asphyxiate. Control with a tourniquet.

A = Airway control. Is your patient's airway clear? If not, use a jaw thrust or head tilt to open their airway. Clear any visible blockages.

R = Respiratory support. Look, listen, and feel for your patient's breath. If they are not breathing, assess the chest wall for trauma and provide artificial breathing.

C = Circulation. Check your patient's pulse and capillary refill. Control any bleeding, reevaluate the tourniquet, if applicable, and determine whether immobilizing the spine is necessary.

H = Hypothermia. Protect your patient from the elements. Keep your patient comfortable, dry, and sheltered.

Once you have completed the M.A.R.C.H. protocol, proceed to care for the patient's injuries.

Make a Splint or Sling

The purpose of a splint or sling is to immobilize a wounded extremity to prevent further injury and reduce pain. If you do not have a SAM (structural aluminum malleable) splint in your kit, improvise with the gear you do have. Trekking

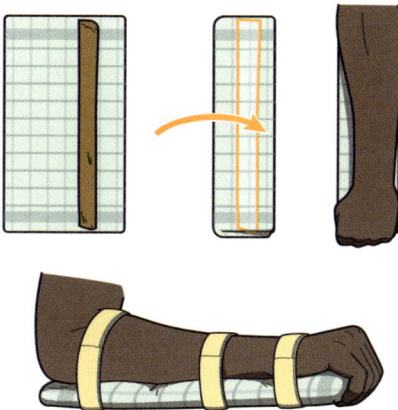

poles or tree branches can be tied on using elastic bandages, scarves, or socks.

When constructing a splint, follow these steps:

1.   When using a SAM splint, the head and neck should be immobilized first if you suspect that the patient has a head, neck, or back injury.

2.   Remove all jewelry from the injured extremity.

3.   Use padding, like extra clothing, towels, or sleeping pads, to make the splint comfortable.

4.   Use sturdy materials to form the splint. Be creative.

5.   The splint should extend well past the bone break or injured joint.

6.   We do not hold our fingers, wrists, ankles, arms, or legs completely straight, so do not splint them this way. Allow a slight, natural bend at affected joints so that the patient is comfortable.

7.   Secure the splint both above and below the injury—but not directly over the injury—with whatever you have available, including belts, socks, T-shirts, or vines. Tie the material securely so that the knots and splints do not slip and so the limb cannot be moved. Do not tie the splint so tightly that blood flow to the limb is reduced.

8. Always check blood flow and sensation beyond the injury and splint to make sure you have not tied the splint too tight or splinted in a restrictive position. Recheck often, and loosen or reposition splints and tie-downs as needed.

Slings can be used to help immobilize fractures, strains, sprains, and dislocations. Create a sling using a jacket, long-sleeved shirt, or scarf.

Set a Bone

If you need more than four hours to reach definitive care, set a broken bone. Otherwise, splint bones in place to hold them in their current position while you transport the patient.

The two types of bone fractures are closed and open. A closed fracture is a break that does not penetrate the skin; an open fracture has punctured tissue and skin to expose the bone, creating an open wound.

Closed Fractures

In most circumstances, an untrained person should not attempt to set a fractured bone. In the rare event that you must do so because of poor or low circulation below the break, follow these steps:

1. Securely hold the limb above the fracture to keep the limb from moving; this step may require the assistance of another person, if available.

2. Grab the limb below the fracture, and straighten the limb by pulling on it. You may or may not hear the bone pop into place, but proper alignment should relieve some pain for your patient.

3. While still holding the limb in place, apply a splint to keep the limb from moving again.

4. Check that the patient can move their other extremities or feel the touch of your hand beyond the fracture.

Open Fractures

Open fractures present great risk for infection. If definitive care can be reached in less than four hours, do not attempt to set the bone. Instead, irrigate the exposed bone ends and cover them with a moist dressing. If definitive care is more than four hours away, irrigate the exposed bone ends and pull them back under the skin prior to bandaging and splinting. If you must set an open fracture, follow these steps:

1. Thoroughly irrigate and clean the wound.

2. Hold the limb above the fracture to keep it from moving; this step may require the assistance of another person.

3. Grab the limb below the fracture, and straighten the limb by pulling on it. Proper alignment should relieve some pain for your patient.

4. While holding the limb in place, apply a splint.

5. Cover the open wound with a sterile dressing or a clean cloth and bandage it.

6. Check that the patient is able to move their other extremities or feel the touch of your hand beyond the fracture. Recheck often.

Femur fractures require immediate attention because significant blood loss is possible.

Pelvic fractures cannot be set and will require immediate evacuation. Secure the fracture in place using a jacket or long-sleeved shirt. Set the patient in a comfortable position and place padding between their legs. With the jacket, tie both legs together to limit motion.

Treat Shock

Shock is the lack of blood flow to vital organs, including the brain. Several causes of shock include:

Cardiogenic shock is due to heart attack or trauma to the heart.

Hypovolemic shock is the result of low fluid levels in the body caused by severe bleeding, dehydration, or burns.

Vasogenic shock is unrestricted blood flow that the heart cannot regulate. Vasogenic shock is typically associated with spinal injuries, infection, or severe allergies.

Septic shock is also related to infection and causes dangerously low blood pressure.

Injuries such as bone breaks and severe bleeding can cause shock, as can witnessing an accident or frightening occurrence. Symptoms of shock are cold, pale, and clammy skin; increased heart and respiration rate; confusion; and altered level of consciousness. As shock progresses, heart rate may slow, respiration may slow, and the pulse may be weak or difficult to find.

When treating shock, begin by addressing the underlying injury if possible: splint fractures, stop bleeding, address allergic reactions, treat burns, and/or clean infected wounds.

Keep the patient warm by covering them with blankets or moving them to a warmer area. In the case of shock due to overheating or exhaustion, protect your patient from the heat and keep them cool.

Elevate the patient's feet about 12 inches above their heart and keep them comfortable and hydrated so long as they can maintain consciousness. Patients suffering from shock should be evacuated as soon as possible.

Stop Bleeding

Though it is important to stop any bleeding, some wounds are more serious than others. Bleeding is classified by the types of vessels that are injured.

Capillary bleeding is the most common type of bleeding and typically arises from a surface wound with the blood slowly oozing. Although you may see a lot of blood at first, these wounds tend to clot on their own.

Venous bleeding can be identified by a steady flow of blood that is maroon or dark in color. These wounds are less likely to clot on their own.

Arterial bleeding can be immediately identified, as blood spurts from the wound under high pressure. Swift treatment is required.

Bleeding can occur externally—blood leaving the body—or internally, with blood pooling in the body. Little can be done in the wilderness for internal bleeds other than stabilizing the injury and keeping the patient warm and comfortable until help arrives.

For external bleeds, apply direct pressure by following these steps:

1. Put gloves on if you have them.

2. Using the heel of your hand, apply direct pressure to the wound for 10 to 20 minutes.

3. Bandage the wound, using sterile bandages whenever possible; otherwise, use what you have to absorb the blood.

4. If the original bandage soaks through with blood, do not remove it. Removing the bandage will remove any clotting that has occurred. Place a new bandage over the top of the old bandage and continue to apply pressure.

5. Raise the wound above the patient's heart whenever possible.

A tourniquet should only be used if direct pressure does not work. A tourniquet can only be used on extremities; do not apply a tourniquet on the chest, abdomen, pelvis, or neck. Always note the time that the tourniquet was applied. Once a tourniquet is applied, it should only be removed by a medical professional in a hospital setting.

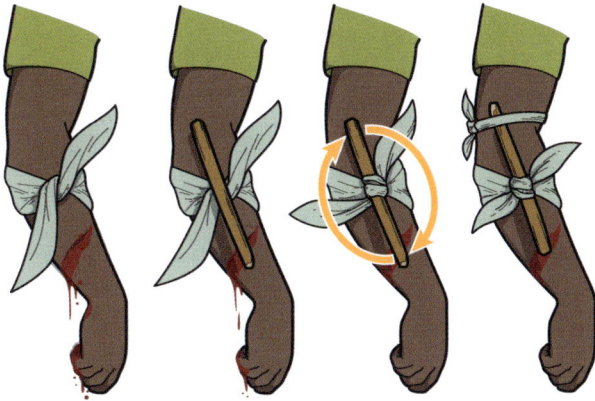

Combat application tourniquets (CATs) and stretch-wrap-and-tuck tourniquets (SWAT-Ts) are available to the public and should be carried in your pack. If you do not have a proper tourniquet, improvise with any material that is at least two inches wide, like a scarf, sock, or thick rope. A belt can be used, but thick cloth is more effective because a proper knot can be tied. The wider the material the better, as wider material causes less localized damage where the tourniquet is applied.

Follow these steps to make and apply a tourniquet:

1. Place the tourniquet or cloth about two inches above the wound but not on a joint. If two inches puts you on a joint, move two inches above the joint, closer to the heart.

2. Tie a secure knot around the extremity.

3. Place a stick on top of the overhand knot and tie another knot around the stick.

4. Twist the stick, thereby tightening the cloth/ bandage, until the bleeding stops. This step will be painful for the patient but is necessary to save their life.

5. Secure the stick so that it will not unravel or cause the tourniquet to come loose.

6. Write down the time the tourniquet was applied, either on the tourniquet itself or on the patient's forehead.

Disinfect a Wound

A wound should be thoroughly cleaned before being dressed and bandaged. Cleaning a wound is known as "irrigation" by emergency response personnel. Irrigation means flushing a wound with high-pressure water to clean out any debris or foreign material. Sterilize the water by filtering and boiling it first. Using dirty water will remove debris but will not disinfect the wound.

Puncture wounds should be soaked or gently flushed rather than irrigated, as irrigation forces debris and bacteria farther into these types of wounds.

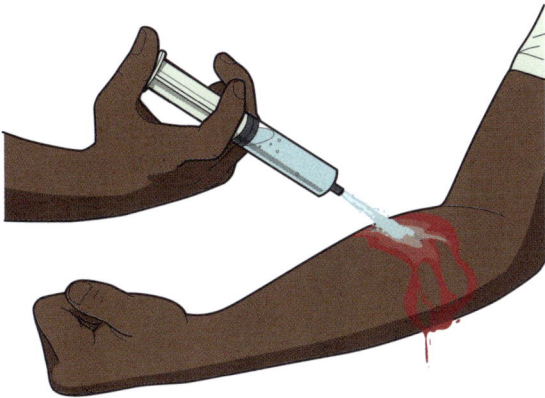

When irrigating a wound, use the following steps:

1. If possible, use a syringe to create a high-pressure stream. Some modern water purifiers come with a syringe to backflush the filter. If a syringe isn't available, poke a tiny hole in the corner of a sandwich bag or other plastic bag, seal the bag tightly, and squeeze it to create a relatively high-pressure stream. Plastic drinking bottles may work as well.

2. Gently open the wound and flush out the inside of the wound as well as surrounding areas. The more water, the better. Continue to flush the wound until all foreign material is removed.

3. If you carry iodine water-purification tablets, you can use them to make a sterile solution to apply to the wound.

4. Once the wound is clean, bandage it to keep it clean.

Bandage a Wound

The purpose of bandaging a wound is to keep it clean, comfortable, and also to pull the edges of the wound together to promote healing. To bandage a wound, follow these steps:

1. After thoroughly cleaning a wound, place a sterile gauze over it.

2. Wrap rolled bandage around the injured extremity or body part until the entire wound is covered and the gauze is covered. If you do not have rolled bandage in your supplies, a scarf, T-shirt, or other clean material will work just fine.

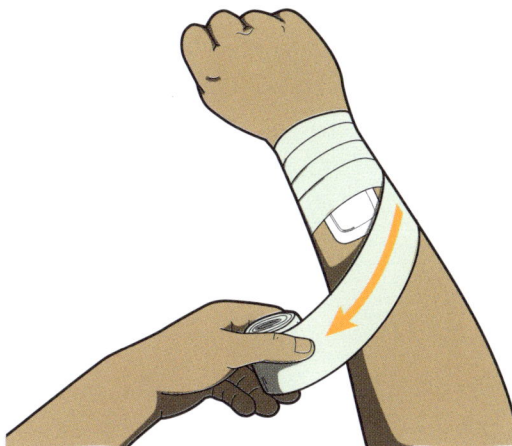

3. Tuck the end of the bandage inside the wrap to secure the bandage in place.

4. Replace the dressing and bandages as needed if blood soaks through, but be careful not to remove any clotted blood, which will cause the injury to start bleeding again. If the dressing sticks to the wound, soak the dressing in water until the bandage pulls away freely.

Sometimes a bandage is not necessary, and tape can be used. Micropore medical tape is a great addition to your kit. Otherwise, use duct tape or electrical tape:

5. Cut the tape into narrow strips (roughly ¼ inch wide and one to two inches long).

6. Place the strips about ¼ inch apart and pull the wound together just so the edges of the wound touch. Do not overtighten. Overtightening will cause discomfort and may prevent proper healing.

7. You may need to trim body hair for the tape to stick properly, but do not shave the area, which could promote infection.

Treat Burns

Immediate medical attention should be administered if your hands, feet, face, or genitalia are burned, or if more than 10 percent of your body is burned. The palm of your hand, not including your fingers, represents 1 percent of your body, making it easy to estimate the percentage of the body that is burned.

Superficial burns (first degree) are typically associated with a mild sunburn. These burns involve reddening of the skin but no blistering. Though they can be very painful, superficial burns are usually easy to treat. Soak the wound in cool water for five minutes to cool the skin and underlying tissue. You may take ibuprofen or other similar painkillers and apply topical anesthetic such as burn cream, aloe, or lidocaine. Wear loose clothing to protect the area.

Partial thickness burns (second degree) are identified by blistering of the skin and skin that is discolored to red, white, or yellow. These burns are extremely painful because deeper layers of skin are damaged. Remove any jewelry or clothing that would be hard to remove should swelling occur.

To treat partial thickness burns, the first step is to cool the area by soaking the wound in cool water for at least 15 minutes. Take painkillers such as ibuprofen, but do not apply topical anesthetic, which will trap heat and cause the burn to worsen. Once the skin is cooled, gently clean the area with a clean cloth and water. Do not burst the blisters, which protect the underlying tissue. It is not unusual for the skin to slough off. After cleaning the area, pat it dry with a clean cloth or gauze before applying a bandage. Apply the bandage loosely so you don't irritate the wound further.

Full thickness burns (third degree) have burned away all layers of the skin, as well as blood vessels and nerves directly under the skin layer. Although the flesh is most likely charred, the patient will feel little to no pain as the nerve endings have been destroyed. Likely, partial thickness burns are also present.

The risks of shock and infection are great with full thickness burns. Flush the skin with cool water to stop the burning process, and remove any jewelry or clothing from the area. Remove dead skin, debris, or foreign material if possible. Provide the patient with a lot of fluids and electrolytes. Bandage the burn loosely to help prevent contamination, further injury, and infection. Definitive medical care should be administered as soon as possible.

Extreme burns (fourth to sixth degree) aren't commonly encountered in the wilderness, but they involve charred muscle, fat, and bone. Loss of limb and life is highly probable. Cool and bandage the wound to the best of your ability and seek immediate medical attention.

Treat Dehydration

Sweating, vomiting, diarrhea, and high altitudes are typical causes of dehydration in wilderness settings. The best way to treat dehydration is to prevent it in the first place by drinking lots of fluids. Signs of dehydration are very dark urine or not urinating at all, dry skin that does not return to its original position when pinched, dizziness, confusion, fever, rapid heartbeat, and unconsciousness.

Should you or someone in your party become dehydrated, move the patient to a cool, shaded area and have them slowly drink water, sports drinks, or clear broth, or suck on ice. If you have loose sugar and/or salt, add small amounts to plain water to replenish electrolytes. A severely dehydrated patient may not be able to hold down fluids if they drink too quickly, but they should consume fluids as quickly as possible. Dehydrated patients who cannot hold down fluids or who are unconscious will need to be evacuated so that they can be administered an IV to rehydrate.

Treat Hypothermia

Hypothermia is the result of your core body temperature dropping below 95°F (35°C). Some common symptoms include uncontrollable shivering, confusion, disorientation, pale and cold skin, and an elevated heart and breathing rate.

Spot hypothermia with the "mumbles, stumbles, and grumbles." If your friend, who doesn't normally have issues talking, walking, or keeping their cool, suddenly starts acting funny, assess them immediately. Another early detection method is to attempt to touch your little finger to your thumb. When hypothermic, your body starts to lose fine motor function. If you cannot touch these fingers together, you are starting to shut down. Finally, if you are shivering uncontrollably and then stop shivering, but nothing has changed to warm you up, severe hypothermia has set in and you need to be warmed immediately.

The best treatment for mild hypothermia is to get out of the cold environment and begin rapid rewarming. Follow these steps:

1. Find a place that is out of the cold and wind.

2. Remove any wet clothing and replace it with dry clothing or wrap yourself or your patient in blankets.

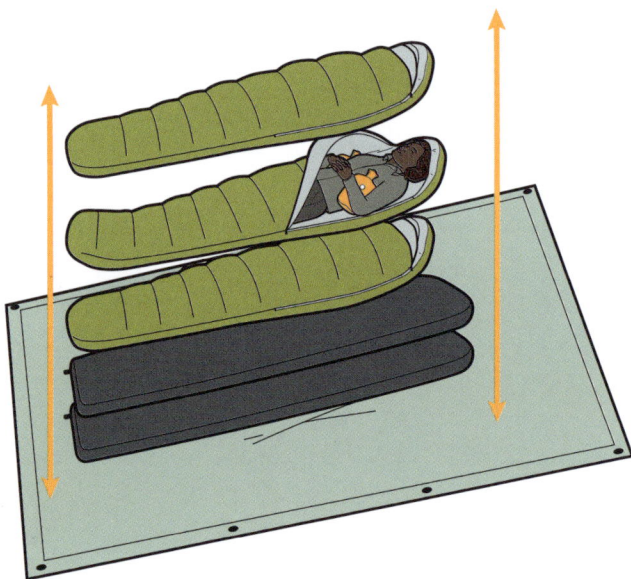

To promote rapid rewarming, create a "thermal burrito," with layers of insulation below and on top of the patient. Place hot water bottles under the armpits or between the thighs.

3. Start a fire, drink warm water, and place a hot water bottle under your armpits or between your thighs. Do not place hot bottles directly against the skin, which could result in a burn. Alcohol and caffeinated drinks should be avoided as they can make the situation worse.

4. If you are able to, try some light exercise like walking or slow jumping jacks to help with the rewarming.

Patients with severe hypothermia may suffer altered mental states including extreme irritability. Ignore their grumbles and provide care. Get them out of the cold and begin rewarming as quickly as possible, but do not let them exercise or overexert themselves. Overexertion can send them into cardiac arrest.

If you fear that your patient has frozen to death, remember the saying "No one is dead until they are warm and dead." Although this saying is a bit morbid, it holds true. A frozen person can and has been brought back to life with no permanent damage.

Treat Altitude Sickness

Varying degrees of altitude sickness occur, but the condition is treated similarly in each case.

AMS = Acute Mountain Sickness is the mildest form of altitude sickness and tends to affect people starting at about

8,000 feet in elevation, though I have seen people experience AMS as low as 6,000 feet. Symptoms include headache, vomiting, fatigue, insomnia, and dizziness. Staying well hydrated is a way to help combat AMS, but the most effective treatment is to descend elevation rapidly until you feel better.

HAPE = High-Altitude Pulmonary Edema is life-threatening and is the result of fluid in the lungs. HAPE typically becomes a concern at over 11,000 feet in elevation, but it has been reported at elevations as low as 8,000 feet. Symptoms are much like AMS but are typically accompanied by a dry cough that can develop and that produces pink or bloody sputum. Oxygen, along with rest, is sometimes administered for mild cases of HAPE. Best practice in the wilderness is to descend until symptoms disappear.

HACE = High-Altitude Cerebral Edema is swelling of the brain with symptoms like AMS and including confusion, disorientation, and lethargy. Any sign of an altered mental status at high elevation (usually over 13,000 feet) should be dealt with quickly. If an individual is experiencing HACE, unlike HAPE or AMS, the person should descend slowly, allowing their body and brain time to acclimatize. The drug dexamethasone can be administered for less severe cases, but in severe cases, the patient should be quickly evacuated to lower elevations and administered oxygen. Left untreated, HACE can kill within 48 hours.

AMS, HAPE, and HACE cannot be slept off. Remember the adage "Hike high, sleep low." Hike to a high elevation during the day, let your body experience the higher elevation, then descend for the night to rest and allow your body to acclimate before continuing higher again.

Treat Bites and Stings

Animal bites. The risk of infection from animal bites is high. If the bite does not break the skin, administer pain medications such as ibuprofen. If the bite breaks the skin, apply direct pressure to stop the bleed, followed by a thorough irrigation and cleaning of the wound, using soap if it is available. Once cleaned, dress the wound with a clean bandage. Monitor the bite closely for infection, and if you suspect the attacking animal had rabies, seek medical attention immediately.

Snakebites. Snakebite envenomation symptoms include severe burning at the bite wound, swelling, blood oozing from the bite, nausea, weakness, numbness of the tongue, difficulty breathing, shock, and increased heart and breathing rates. Many inaccurate myths exist about treating snakebites. You cannot suck out the venom, and you should not open a snakebite to bleed it out. Do not apply ice or use a tourniquet. Do not administer aspirin. Instead, take the following steps:

1. Remain calm and keep physical activity to a minimum to prevent venom from rapidly spreading throughout the body.

2. Remove tight-fitting clothing and jewelry in case of swelling.

3. Immobilize and elevate the bite wound to the same level as the heart.

4. Evacuate the patient to definitive care.

Stings. Bees, wasps, ants, and scorpions are common sources of stings in the wilderness. Bees typically can only sting you once, but wasps, ants, and scorpions can sting you multiple times.

If a stung person is allergic and has been prescribed epinephrine injections, administer their approved dosage and evacuate them immediately. If any person develops shortness of breath or other difficulties in breathing, they should be evacuated and seek immediate medical attention.

If the stung person does not develop any unusual swelling or breathing difficulties, monitor them for a while. While monitoring them, clean the sting site with soap and water and apply a cool compress to reduce pain and swelling. Pain medications can also be administered.

NATURAL REMEDIES

Many plants can be used for minor wound or illness care. Some plants require processing to make salves or tinctures, whereas other plants can be used directly. Remember to consider the patient's allergies before using any plant. Study up on the medicinal use of plants native to your area. Here are three wild plants that I use:

Yarrow. Crush flowers and leaves of the yarrow plant and apply the poultice to a wound to stop bleeding. Yarrow can also be used to relieve menstrual pain.

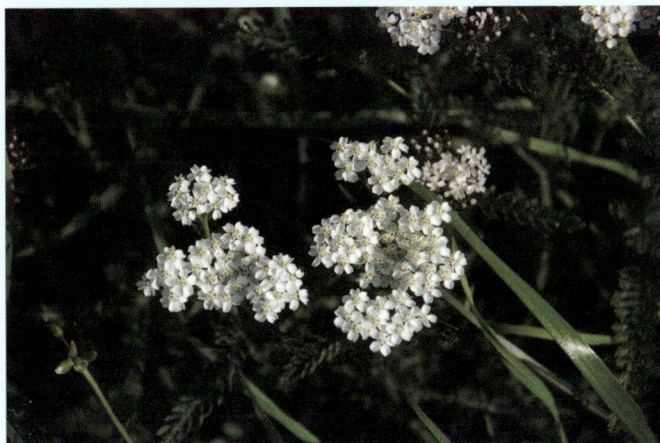

Plantain. Apply crushed plantain leaves to wounds, insect bites, or stings to provide anti-inflammatory relief. Eat the leaves and seeds or prepare a tea to help soothe stomach pains related to ulcers, diarrhea, or constipation.

Pine sap. Apply pine sap directly to wounds, cuts, sores, and burns to promote healing. Pine sap is anti-inflammatory and antiseptic, and helps seal wounds. If the sap is dry or crystalized, heat it slightly before applying to the wound.

RESOURCES

Books

Alton, Joseph D., and Amy E. Alton. *The Survival Medicine Handbook: The Essential Guide for When Help Is Not on the Way.* Weston, FL: Doom and Bloom LLC, 2016.

Arora, David. *All That the Rain Promises, and More: A Hip Pocket Guide to Western Mushrooms.* Berkeley, CA: Ten Speed Press, 1991.

Moore, Michael. *Medicinal Plants of the Mountain West: A Guide to the Identification, Preparation, and Uses of Traditional Medicinal Plants Found in the Mountains, Foothills, and Upland Areas of the American West.* Santa Fe, NM: Museum of New Mexico Press, 1979.

Williams, Scott B. *Bug Out: The Complete Plan for Escaping a Catastrophic Disaster Before It's Too Late.* Berkeley, CA: Ulysses Press, 2010.

Websites

AnimatedKnots.com

MyTopo.com

NOAA.gov

USGS.gov

GLOSSARY

Arbor knot: A slip knot used to secure or compress a load such as a sleeping bag, or the first knot to create a lashing

Azimuth: Used in land navigation, a horizontal angle measured clockwise from a north baseline

Bearing block: The piece of a bow drill set used to hold the drill in place, which also allows the user to apply a significant amount of downward pressure on the drill

Bird's nest: A bundle of dry, fine, natural materials fashioned into the shape of a bird's nest, used to start a fire

Bow drill set: A drill worked by means of a bow and string, commonly used to start fires or drill holes through wood; comprised of a fireboard, drill, bearing block, ember pan, and a crude bow

Bowline knot: A knot used to form a loop that neither slips nor jams

Bushcraft: Wilderness survival by means of using materials and resources from the natural environment; a bushcrafter uses primitive skills and natural materials as a means of survival or as a hobby while enjoying the outdoors

Clove hitch: An easily releasable knot temporarily securing a rope to an object; commonly used to start lashings or to run cordage along a series of posts

Contour lines: Lines on a map joining points of equal height above or below sea level

Cow hitch: Also called the lark's head knot; used to attach rope to an object, an excellent locking knot for animal traps and snares

Deadfall trap: A trap consisting of a heavy weight, positioned to fall on an animal, and a trigger mechanism

Declination: The deviation of the compass from True North

Fatwood: Also known as fat lighter or lighter wood; a dense, highly water-resistant, and highly flammable material derived from sap- and resin-impregnated wood found in pine trees, especially damaged or dead trees

Featherstick: A length of wood that is shaved to produce a cluster of thin curls protruding from the wood allowing wood to more easily start on fire

Ferrocerium rod: A metallic rod used to start fires; when scraped with a hard, sharp edge, the rod produces sparks in excess of 3,000 degrees Fahrenheit

Fireboard: Also known as a hearthboard; the piece of a bow drill set in which the drill spins to generate wood ash that will heat up and combust

Fire lay: A small, strategically placed structure made of sticks, tinder, kindling and other easily ignitable material to facilitate the ignition of a fire

Frapping: A binding used to create a tight, secure juncture by pinching together two or more lengths of rope that are currently lashed to each other

Full-tang knife: A knife that is one solid piece from the tip of the blade to the end of the handle; two-handle pieces are pinned on to the blade, one on each side

Kindling: Easily combustible sticks, twigs, or other materials used for starting a fire

Knife spine: The back side of the knife opposite the blade

Lashing: A cord used to fasten objects, typically poles, securely together

Magnetic North: A varying point on the surface of Earth's Northern Hemisphere at which the planet's magnetic field points vertically downward

Paracord: A lightweight nylon rope, originally used for the suspension lines of parachutes; typically made up of an outer braided sheath and seven internal strands and is rated to hold 550 pounds of weight

Poacher's knot: A knot that forms an adjustable loop, mainly used for binding a rope to an object; also known as a double overhand noose

Siberian hitch: A slipped hitch knot, easy to tie while wearing gloves; commonly used as a quick-release knot to secure rope ridgelines for tarp shelters

Snare trap: A trap made of wire, rope, or natural plant fibers, having a noose at one end to capture birds or small animals

Square knot: A symmetrical double knot that holds securely and is easy to untie; commonly used to join two ends of a rope together

True North: The North Pole; north according to Earth's axis

IMAGE INDEX

INDEX

S

W

Wasps, 139, 186
Water
    in arid climates, 45–46
    capturing, 69–70
    contamination, 49
    filtration, 27–28, 70–71
    hydration kits, 20, 26–28
    importance of, 68
    locating, 69
    purification, 26–28, 70–72
    The Rule of Threes, 7
Weather. *See also* Climates
    checking, 10
    preparing for unexpected, 51
Wild animals
    bears, 132–134
    bites, 185
    coyotes, 135–136
    deer/elk/moose, 138
    mountain lions, 134–135
    snakes, 46–47, 136–138
Wounds
    bandaging, 176–178
    disinfecting, 175–176

Y

Yarrow, 187

ACKNOWLEDGMENTS

I picked up so many things through the years, not by reading books by big names, but by living with awesome, everyday mountain people. My first mentors were my family. My father taught me how to hunt, fish, listen to the forest, and see what most people pass by. He helped me build my first tree fort, and though that fort is no longer standing, a survival camp classroom stands in its location today. My mother taught me cooking, sewing, basic first aid, herbal remedies, how to be creative, and how to treat people with respect. My quirky and independent sister taught me it's okay to follow your dreams.

My other mentors include:

Griz, who lived in a single-room cabin in the mountains. Griz always smelled of campfire and sweat, with a dirty face, big scruffy beard, kind eyes, and a big smile.

My uncle Michael Richardson, who adventured with my father and has probably climbed every 14er in Colorado at least a dozen times.

My dad's friend Monte Barrett, the unsung hero of Pikes Peak, who helped save Barr Camp and took us hiking into secret places on the mountain.

My science teacher Mr. Crane, who worked at Rocky Mountain National Park and shared stories of his crazy adventures.

My dad's military friends—guys with names like Big Dog, Little Dog, Scruff, Jumps, Razz, One Eyed Chuck, Wildman, and Snake. They all had valuable lessons to teach me and probably thought I wasn't listening. But I was.

Doug Philpy, who worked at the dump and taught me that you can make tools out of anything.

Jim Birmingham, who taught me how to speak in public, tell stories, and how to properly bank a fire so that it will last untouched all night.

Mike Parker, who taught me how to be a leader. He showed me this crazy thing called the Internet and later helped me get an IT job, which, many years later, allowed me to launch my survival business.

My best friend Robin Schneider, who made me realize that life is too short not to follow your dreams. Robin almost died from cancer, but he fought through, and when he came out the other side, he changed his life.

ABOUT THE AUTHOR

Jason Marsteiner is the owner of Colorado Mountain Man Survival LLC and The Survival University (TheSurvivalUniversity.com). Since 2010, he has been training individuals, families, corporate leaders, and military personnel including Special Forces in the art of modern and primitive wilderness survival. Jason has spent much of his life learning and improving these life-saving techniques.

At The Survival University, located in the mountains of Colorado, he offers over 60 courses throughout the year and has developed his own comprehensive training program, the 50-Day Wilderness Immersion. Students learn a robust variety of skills from experts in advanced-skills training from all over the country.

NOTES

_____

_____

_____

_____

_____

_____

_____

_____

_____

_____

_____

_____

_____

_____

_____

_____

_____